CAMPAIGN 374

THE BATTLE OF GETTYSBURG 1863 (1)

The First Day

TIMOTHY J. ORR

ILLUSTRATED BY STEVE NOON
Series editor Nikolai Bogdanovic

OSPREY PUBLISHING
Bloomsbury Publishing Plc
Kemp House, Chawley Park, Cumnor Hill, Oxford OX2 9PH, UK
29 Earlsfort Terrace, Dublin 2, Ireland
1385 Broadway, 5th Floor, New York, NY 10018, USA
E-mail: info@ospreypublishing.com
www.ospreypublishing.com

OSPREY is a trademark of Osprey Publishing Ltd

First published in Great Britain in 2022

A catalog record for this book is available from the British Library.

ISBN: PB 9781472848499; eBook 9781472848390; ePDF 9781472848406;
XML 9781472848413

22 23 24 25 26   10 9 8 7 6 5 4 3 2 1

Maps by Bounford.com
3D BEVs by Paul Kime
Index by Janet Andrew
Typeset by PDQ Digital Media Solutions, Bungay, UK
Printed and bound in India by Replika Press Private Ltd.

MIX
Paper from
responsible sources
FSC® C016779
FSC
www.fsc.org

Artist's note

Readers may care to note that the original paintings from which the color
plates in this book were prepared are available for private sale. All
reproduction copyright whatsoever is retained by the publishers. The artist
can be contacted via the following website:

https://www.steve-noon.co.uk

The publishers regret that they can enter into no correspondence upon
this matter.

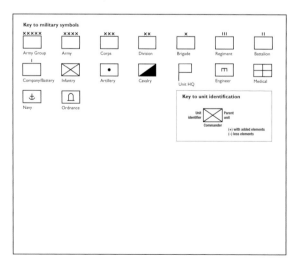

Photographic images

All of the photographs that appear in this work are Public Domain.

Osprey Publishing supports the Woodland Trust, the UK's leading woodland
conservation charity.

To find out more about our authors and books visit
www.ospreypublishing.com. Here you will find extracts, author
interviews, details of forthcoming events and the option to sign up for
our newsletter.

TITLE PAGE:
A photograph of Gettysburg taken on July 7, 1863, looking north
from the roof of the Evergreen Cemetery, which sits atop the crest of
Cemetery Hill. (Library of Congress)

CONTENTS

ORIGINS OF THE CAMPAIGN

The Gettysburg Campaign began with a letter.

On May 9, 1863, Robert E. Lee, the commander of the Army of Northern Virginia, received a troubling message from his Secretary of War, James Seddon. The Confederate cabinet secretary recommended that Lee prepare to detach "two or three brigades" and send them to the support of the besieged Mississippi River Theater. Seddon's dispatch caused Lee unease. Fiercely covetous of his authority, he had no desire to see his army—an army he had molded, honed, and disciplined over the course of the past eleven months—carved up and loaned to other officers. Often hidebound in his strategic outlook, Lee believed he could accomplish more if he kept his army intact than by detaching parts of it across all theaters of the Confederacy.

Any other commander might have appreciated the urgency in sparing troops to protect the Confederacy's other embattled theaters, where the strategic situation teetered precariously. Already, Union forces under Maj. Gen. Ulysses S. Grant had landed on the east bank of the Mississippi. As the next few days transpired, Grant's army took the state capital at Jackson. By the end of the month, his army encircled the vital garrison at Vicksburg, cutting off more than 30,000 rebel soldiers. Meanwhile, another Union army—Maj. Gen. Nathaniel P. Banks's Army of the Gulf—was moving to surround Port Hudson, a Confederate bastion on the lower Mississippi. If the Confederacy lost these two positions, President Jefferson Davis could all but write-off support from the trans-Mississippi states.

Meanwhile, a sizable Union army under Maj. Gen. William S. Rosecrans (56,000 troops) was quartered outside of Murfreesboro, Tennessee. Poised to make a march against the indispensable rail hub at Chattanooga, this army planned to complete its conquest of Tennessee by the end of the summer. The loss of Chattanooga would, in effect, open the way for an invasion of the Deep South. Yet another Union army—of 20,000 troops—garrisoned another important rail hub at Suffolk, preventing the Confederacy from regaining control of the

The fourth Confederate Secretary of War, James Seddon, initially wanted to send two or three of Lee's brigades to the Western Theater. After a meeting with the Confederate cabinet, Seddon became convinced that Lee's plan to invade Pennsylvania was a better course of action. (NARA)

A former U.S. Secretary of War and a former U.S. Senator from Mississippi, Jefferson Davis led the Confederacy as its Commander-in-Chief. Thin-skinned and petty, he despised high-ranking Confederate officers who offered him strategic advice. But Lee was not one of them. When Lee suggested leading the Army of Northern Virginia into Pennsylvania, Davis offered his wholesale support. (Library of Congress)

Virginia Tidewater. In April, a Confederate corps commander, Lieut. Gen. James Longstreet, had attempted to drive out these intruders, but by the end of the month, the bluecoats remained in place. Finally, the U.S. Navy's South Atlantic Squadron under Rear Adm. Samuel Du Pont had blockaded Charleston. Although Confederate forces had repelled Du Pont's warships in a highly publicized battle on April 7, a corps of Union infantry under Maj. Gen. David Hunter began hopscotching its way across the harbor islands, intent on laying siege to Charleston's land batteries. All across the continent, Union forces were poised to take several large bites out of the Confederacy.

The Confederacy's only bright spot sparkled in upper Virginia. Although at high cost, the Army of Northern Virginia had recently defeated the Army of the Potomac in a series of battles known as the Chancellorsville Campaign. After losing some 17,300 men killed, wounded, or captured, the Union army retired across the Rappahannock River, shamed by its defeat. Not mincing words, a critical newspaper editor from New Jersey commented, "Once more the gallant Army of the Potomac, controlled by an imbecile department and led by an incompetent general, has been marched to fruitless slaughter."

Within days, the Union disaster at Chancellorsville earned the Confederate government important political dividends. Over the previous winter, the North's Democratic Party had mobilized a peace faction known as the Copperheads. Deeply racist, the Copperheads found it outrageous that white citizens were forced to fight and die for the cause of Emancipation. Now, after Chancellorsville, some of them began murmuring pleas for an armistice, a peaceful resolution to the war without sectional reunification. So wrote one Philadelphia Copperhead: "Peace, peace, *on any terms*, at any price: anything to end this fratricidal war."

Cast against this political backdrop, Lee believed the Army of Northern Virginia could not stand idle while a political opportunity confronted it, nor could it stand to lose any additional men through transfer to other theaters. Already, the tabulated casualty figures from Chancellorsville painted a depressing picture. During the previous week, the Army of Northern Virginia had sustained 13,640 losses—twenty-two percent of its total. If more troops departed, so Lee complained, he could not carry out any offensive operations. Taking stock of his intelligence reports, Lee supposed his army was "greatly outnumbered." In fact, he estimated that some 159,000 federal soldiers occupied Virginia. "You can therefore see," Lee wrote to Secretary of War Seddon the day after receiving the letter about potential troop transfers, "the odds against us decide whether the line of Virginia is more in danger than the line of the Mississippi." Acting quickly to avoid dissection of his army, Lee fired off a letter to President Davis, requesting a meeting. Promptly, Davis invited Lee to consult with him in Richmond.

Lee journeyed to the capital on May 14. In addition to Davis and Seddon, he met with other members of the Confederate cabinet, and while in conversation with them, he shared an idea that had been percolating for the past four months. Lee believed he should lead his army in an offensive operation on the north side of the Potomac River. On the level of national strategy, Lee was tired of having his army act defensively. The time had come, he said, for the Army of Northern Virginia to invade the United States.

Postmaster-General John H. Reagan was the only member of the Confederate cabinet to describe the substance of the May 15 meeting with Robert E. Lee. A Texan, Reagan feared what might befall the Trans-Mississippi Theater if Lee's invasion failed. After the cabinet approved Lee's plan, Reagan returned to his residence in an unhappy state of mind. He recollected, "I believed we had made a great mistake." (Library of Congress)

At no point during any of his various meetings in Richmond did Lee define his goals, but he must have believed that an invasion would lead to a pivotal, war-concluding engagement, or at the very least, he supposed it would have forced the United States to redeploy troops to counter his incursion. In speaking with Postmaster-General John H. Reagan, Lee began arguing that supplies in Virginia had grown scarce, while forage was much better in Pennsylvania. And then, he blurted out a sentence that laid bare his unbridled confidence in being able to defeat the Army of the Potomac on its home soil. Reagan later recollected, Lee said he "favored such a campaign because he believed he commanded an invincible army, which had been victorious in so many great battles, and in all of them against greatly preponderating numbers and resources."

On May 16, without Lee, the Confederate cabinet held an all-day meeting to discuss the general's proposal. Reagan alone opposed Lee's plan, arguing that it would not likely gain the Confederacy any strategic leverage. The situation along the Mississippi had become critical. Reinforcements from Virginia needed to board trains immediately if they were to have any hope of tipping the scales at Vicksburg. To that end, Reagan insisted that 25,000 or 30,000 of Lee's soldiers be sent to reinforce Maj. Gen. Joseph Johnston's army in Mississippi. However, the other members of the cabinet had been swayed by their conversations with Lee. An invasion of Maryland and Pennsylvania might offset whatever gains Union troops could make along the Mississippi River. Although Reagan objected to that logic, all the other members of the cabinet—and President Davis himself—agreed with Lee's plan. His army, Davis said, should "cross the Potomac, threaten Washington, Baltimore, and Philadelphia." The garrison at Vicksburg would have to hold out without assistance.

No single official document ever described Lee's *specific* reasons for wanting to invade Pennsylvania. His perfunctory after-action report—issued in two parts on July 31, 1863, and in January 1864— said very little. Using passive voice, he argued that the Richmond government agreed with him. Transferring the "scene of hostilities beyond the Potomac," he wrote, was the Confederacy's best move. An invasion might produce "valuable results."

But what did Lee mean by "valuable results"? Several letters offer clues. Earlier in the year, in letters to Davis and Seddon, Lee supposed that crossing the Potomac would relieve pressure on the Confederacy's other beleaguered armies—those at Vicksburg, those in Tennessee, and those in Charleston. However, at the time, Lee worried the roads in Virginia would be too poor to conduct a lengthy campaign. But now, with summer weather drying out the Shenandoah Valley, Lee could maneuver with alacrity. Then, in another letter, on June 10, Lee wrote to Davis suggesting that an invasion of northern territory might convince war-weary U.S. citizens to sue for peace. Lee theorized that a Confederate triumph during the northern political season might tip the scales. He concluded, "It seems to me that the most effectual mode of accomplishing this object, now within our reach, is to give all encouragement we can, consistently with truth, to the rising peace party of the North."

Whatever Lee's reasons—disrupting Union plans for the summer, sparing southern farmers another rough military campaign, or encouraging the northern peace movement—all involved one thing: the execution of a decisive battle. No matter how he dressed up the long-term goals of the campaign to suit Richmond's politicians, Lee needed to fight the Army of the Potomac, defeat it, and reap the fruits of that victory. Quite likely, Postmaster Reagan had read Lee's mind. No general could have envisioned such a path to victory if he did not truly believe in the myth of his army's invincibility. It is not trite to repeat what other historians concluded long ago: Lee's overconfidence was the proximate reason why he fought a battle at Gettysburg and why he lost it.

Although the forces of the United States enjoyed tremendous military success across all theaters of action, by the summer of 1863, Abraham Lincoln had grown frustrated with the lack of progress in Virginia. Repeatedly, Lincoln offered military advice to the Army of the Potomac's commander, Maj. Gen. Joseph Hooker. On June 10, Lincoln advised Hooker to "Fight [Lee] when opportunity offers. If he stays where he is, fret him, and fret him." This photograph of Lincoln was taken on April 17, 1863. (National Portrait Gallery)

CHRONOLOGY

1863

May 15	Lee Meets the Confederate cabinet in Richmond.
June 7–10	Longstreet's and Ewell's corps leave encampments around Culpeper Court House.
June 9	Battle of Brandy Station.
June 14	Hill's corps leaves encampments near Fredericksburg.
June 15	Battle of (Second) Winchester.
June 17	Stuart's cavalry breaks off near Aldie.
June 19	Ewell's corps crosses the Potomac River.
June 20–21	Ewell's corps enters Pennsylvania.
June 24	Hill's corps crosses the Potomac.
June 25	Hill's corps enters Pennsylvania.
June 26	Longstreet's corps crosses the Potomac.
June 27	Longstreet's corps enters Pennsylvania.
June 27	Hooker submits letter of resignation.
June 28	Meade assumes command.
June 28–29	Ewell's reconnaissance toward York and Wrightsville.
June 30	Lee orders concentration of the army.
June 30	Battle of Hanover.
July 1	Battle of Gettysburg.
	7 a.m.: The first shots are fired.
	7 a.m.–10 a.m.: Heth's division drives Buford's division.
	10 a.m.–11.15 a.m.: The morning engagement.
	2.15 p.m.–4.15 p.m.: Rodes's division attacks Robinson's division at Oak Ridge.
	3.15 p.m.–4 p.m.: Heth's division attacks the Union 1st Corps at McPherson's Ridge.
	3.30 p.m.–4 p.m.: Confederate troops attack the 11th Corps.
	4 p.m.–4.30 p.m.: Pender's division attacks Seminary Ridge.
	4.10 p.m.: The Army of the Potomac retreats to Cemetery Hill.

Sixty-nine-year-old John Lawrence Burns served as Gettysburg's constable. During the War of 1812 he had served with the 21st Infantry and participated in the Battle of Lundy's Lane. On July 1, 1863, he put on a high silk hat, grabbed his flintlock, filled his pockets with ammunition, and journeyed to Union lines. There, he met the colonel of the 150th Pennsylvania and asked permission to join the ranks. Col. Langhorne Wister allowed Burns to fight, but advised him to do it from Herbst Woods, as the trees would provide shade and protection. During the afternoon engagement, Burns was wounded three times and retreating Union soldiers had to leave him on the field. The next day, Burns crawled to the edge of town, where a neighbor found him and gave him shelter. Newspapers published his story, lauding him as the "Hero of Gettysburg." Burns recovered from his wounds and died in 1872. (Library of Congress)

THE INVASION OF PENNSYLVANIA

Over the course of May, Lee assembled his army near Culpeper Court House, thirteen miles west of the Rappahannock River, even recalling Lieut. Gen. Longstreet's errant corps from the Siege of Suffolk. Although numbers are not precise, between his various commands, Lee assembled more than 70,000 officers and men. On June 3, he ordered his corps commanders to prepare for the march. It did not take long for Lee's soldiers to know that a great campaign was about to begin. Even without explicit information, the rank-and-file read their commander's mind with astonishing precision. A South Carolinian in McLaws's division wrote to his sister, "A great movement is now on hand. Nearly all the army is here and is cooking up rations to move on. Lee is concentrating a very large army, and 'tis generally believed that he intends attacking the enemy and then march[ing] directly for Pennsylvania." During the second week of June, Lee's soldiers quietly abandoned their camps and began tramping over dusty roads, crossing into the Shenandoah Valley through Ashby's, Snicker's, and Manassas Gaps. One corps, Lieut. Gen. A. P. Hill's, remained downriver near Fredericksburg to convince Union scouts that the bulk of the army had not yet abandoned the line of the Rappahannock.

It did not take long for Union forces to suspect that something was up. When five Confederate divisions abandoned the shores of the Rappahannock on June 3, 4, and 5, the Army of the Potomac's pickets took notice. The army commander, Maj. Gen. Joseph Hooker, determined that these missing enemy troops must be headed to Culpeper. However, Hooker could not tell if Lee's army was simply changing camps or if it was commencing a larger operation. Hoping that a probing action would gather more information, Hooker ordered his cavalry corps (11,000 troops) to cross the upper Rappahannock River at Beverly's and Kelly's fords. He gave his horsemen orders to advance on Culpeper and "disperse or destroy the rebel force in the vicinity." Although Hooker never explained what size force he expected to find, his orders clearly assumed the two fords would be unguarded and that any enemy units in the area would be rear-echelon forces, easily routed.

At dawn, June 9, covered by a thick mist, Union horsemen splashed across the fords and overran the Confederate pickets. Believing they were on the cusp of an easy victory, the Union cavalry pursued the retreating sentries, but they soon found themselves unable to complete their mission. As they broke into the open country southwest of the river, the horsemen saw no rear-echelon contingent. Instead, the region between the Rappahannock River and Culpeper was covered by five brigades belonging to the Confederate cavalry

The Gettysburg Campaign, June 3–July 1, 1863

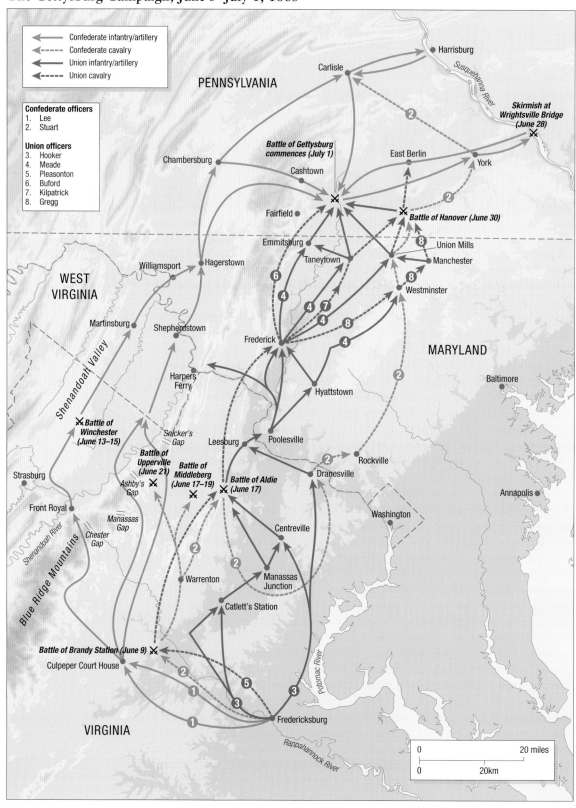

Legend:
- Confederate infantry/artillery
- Confederate cavalry
- Union infantry/artillery
- Union cavalry

Confederate officers
1. Lee
2. Stuart

Union officers
3. Hooker
4. Meade
5. Pleasonton
6. Buford
7. Kilpatrick
8. Gregg

PENNSYLVANIA

Harrisburg

Carlisle

Skirmish at Wrightsville Bridge (June 28)

Chambersburg

Battle of Gettysburg commences (July 1)

Cashtown

East Berlin

York

Fairfield

Battle of Hanover (June 30)

Emmitsburg

Taneytown

Union Mills

Manchester

WEST VIRGINIA

Williamsport

Hagerstown

Westminster

Martinsburg

Shepherdstown

MARYLAND

Frederick

Baltimore

Harpers Ferry

Battle of Winchester (June 13–15)

Snicker's Gap

Hyattstown

Battle of Upperville (June 21)

Ashby's Gap

Battle of Middleberg (June 17–19)

Leesburg

Poolesville

Rockville

Strasburg

Battle of Aldie (June 17)

Dranesville

Front Royal

Manassas Gap

Chester Gap

Washington

Annapolis

Shenandoah River

Blue Ridge Mountains

Centreville

Warrenton

Manassas Junction

Catlett's Station

Potomac River

Battle of Brandy Station (June 9)

Culpeper Court House

VIRGINIA

Fredericksburg

Rappahannock River

0   20 miles
0   20km

10

division, about 10,000 troopers total. Although the Union cavalry commander, Maj. Gen. Alfred Pleasonton, could have ordered a tactical withdrawal in the face of these unexpected odds, he expressed himself eager to "pitch in." Consequently, he allowed a general engagement to take place.

All along their line, the rebel troopers were caught by surprise. Many of them were fatigued by a daylong "grand review" held the day before; yet, despite their exhaustion, they rushed into their saddles and charged into the fray. Complicating the situation, the Confederate cavalry commander, Maj. Gen. James E. B. Stuart, was not present when the fighting initially broke out. Couriers had to dash across the countryside to fetch him. For about ten hours, the so-called Battle of Brandy Station swirled around Stevensburg and Fleetwood Hill. By early afternoon, Pleasonton realized he could not advance farther without endangering his whole command. He ordered his cavalry to withdraw across the fords. By the end of the day, Union forces counted up over 860 losses. The Confederates tallied another 523.

On June 9, 1863, the Army of the Potomac's cavalry corps commander, Maj. Gen. Alfred Pleasonton, initiated the first engagement of the Gettysburg Campaign by ordering his horsemen to cross the Rappahannock River and raid what he assumed to be the Army of Northern Virginia's rear. Pleasonton's cavalry met the Confederate cavalry division in a fierce battle near Brandy Station. By 8 p.m., all Union forces were in retreat, re-crossing the river. After the battle, in his typically self-important manner, Pleasonton reported that he had, for all practical purposes, beaten the enemy. (NARA)

Ultimately, the cavalry engagement at Brandy Station caused Hooker to draw an incorrect conclusion about Lee's intentions. Because Pleasonton's cavalry had been unable to reach Culpeper and had not encountered any enemy wagon trains, the Army of the Potomac's high command assumed that Lee's army was not on the move. Hooker misread the presence of Stuart's division along the upper Rappahannock by concluding that it had been in the process of assembling a large cavalry raid. Although Hooker's pickets continued to report abandoned campsites along the lower Rappahannock, Hooker deluded himself into believing that the bulk of Lee's infantry was still near Fredericksburg. (Further, a misinformed report from a balloon reconnaissance mission conducted from Stafford Heights added weight to this belief.) Generally, Hooker liked this news. With Confederate cavalry upriver, he believed the time was ripe to try another advance. In a letter written to Lincoln dated June 10, Hooker hinted that he intended to use this opportunity to move south and capture Richmond. Doubting the accuracy of Hooker's conclusions, Lincoln responded with an admonition: stay put until further notice.

With Hooker unaware of Lee's intentions, the Army of Northern Virginia stole a march into the Shenandoah Valley. The Confederate infantry moved away in groups. Lieut. Gen. Richard S. Ewell's 2nd Corps moved first, striking tents on June 10. Longstreet's 1st Corps soon followed and all of its troops were en route to the valley by June 15. Finally, Lieut. Gen. A. P. Hill's 3rd Corps began moving the day after that, giving up its encampments along the Rappahannock. From whatever location they started, Lee's men advanced toward Winchester, a town held by a 6,500-man Union garrison commanded by Maj. Gen. Robert Milroy. Lee instructed his vanguard commander, Lieut. Gen. Ewell, to deal with Milroy's men and liberate the city. With 19,000 men—a three-to-one advantage—Ewell crafted a cunning plan. He dispatched one division against a fort that protected Winchester's western side, while another division positioned itself to the northeast, astride Milroy's line of retreat.

In Washington, President Lincoln formed a clear picture of Lee's movements—clearer than Hooker, anyway, who still believed that Lee's army was entrenched along the Rappahannock. Within days of the Confederate infantry's departure from Culpeper, Union outposts near Front Royal detected

The Battle of Brandy Station witnessed the clash of 20,000 Union and Confederate horsemen. Although C.S. cavalry had clearly won the day, critics blamed Maj. Gen. J. E. B. Stuart for allowing the Union cavalry to cross the river in the first place. This 1864 illustration by Edwin Forbes depicts a chaotic scene as Union and Confederate cavalry clashed with sabers. (Library of Congress)

On June 13–15, 1863, Confederate forces under Lieut. Gen. Richard Ewell assaulted the Union garrison at Winchester, forcing Maj. Gen. Robert Milroy to perform a hasty evacuation. In 1863, Winchester numbered approximately 4,400 residents, an even mix of unionists and secessionists. This sketch done by artist Edwin Forbes depicts Winchester as seen from a hill northeast of town. Union forces held a line of forts in the middle distance (and slightly to the right of the city). During their nighttime retreat, Union forces passed across the right foreground of the image. (Library of Congress)

the approach of Ewell's corps. It did not take long for Lincoln and his General-in-Chief, Henry W. Halleck, to sense a crisis brewing. With the bulk of Hooker's army at Stafford Heights, no portion of it could rush to the defense of the Winchester garrison. Fearing the worst, Halleck instructed Milroy to abandon the city and move his forces northward to Harpers Ferry. However, Milroy thought he knew better. Confident that his entrenchments could withstand a Confederate attack, no matter how large, Milroy refused to evacuate. Halleck was furious. He saw no reason to sacrifice a whole division to defend a strategically inconsequential town. On June 14, Halleck ordered Milroy's immediate superior, Maj. Gen. Robert Schenck, to repeat his order. If the garrison did not withdraw immediately, Schenck had orders to relieve Milroy.

By that point, it did not matter. That same day, Ewell's men reached Winchester and encircled the town. In the afternoon, under a flag of truce, Ewell sent a courier to Union lines. He carried the message that all Union troops must lay down their arms and surrender. With bluster, Milroy refused. (According to a popular story, he told the courier to "Go to Hell!") With that, Ewell commenced the battle. His artillery pummeled the federal line with a furious barrage, and late in the evening, a brigade of Louisiana troops overran West Fort and began heading for the city. The Confederate advance stopped only when night prevented it from going farther.

After dark, Milroy reconsidered his situation. Wisely—albeit belatedly—he ordered a retreat. Spiking their artillery, Milroy's soldiers trudged northward along the main road, clumsily navigating their way through the darkness. At first, it appeared as if they might escape the jaws of destruction, but in the morning, near Stephenson's Depot, another of Ewell's divisions attacked the retreating column. Milroy's men stampeded in panic. Those Union soldiers not rounded up by the Confederates scattered into the countryside. Ewell's soldiers corralled 4,000 prisoners, two dozen artillery pieces, and over 300 horses and wagons. Confederate troops plundered the Union forts and received accolades from the city's Confederate citizens. Having been living under federal occupation for the past six months, many Winchester residents were ecstatic. One woman wrote, "It was a day worth living for."

The Union disaster at Winchester shook the United States to its core. Every citizen could now see that Lee's army intended to invade. Lincoln responded

swiftly. On June 15, he called for the states of Maryland, Pennsylvania, West Virginia, and Ohio to raise 100,000 "Emergency Militia" to serve for six months. (A few days later, he asked New York to provide an additional 20,000.) Further, Pennsylvania's governor, Andrew Curtin, called up 50,000 of the Commonwealth's militia to serve under state authority for the next ninety days. Excitement prevailed inside cities along the border—Baltimore, Harrisburg, and Washington, D.C. Citizens stood glued to their bulletin boards or they crowded around newspaper offices, wondering which city would be the rebels' first target. Wild reports kept everyone on edge. One Baltimore editor complained that "extravagant rumors" of all kinds arrived "so various in form and fast succeeding each other in number that it would be fruitless to expose or contradict any particular one."

In the states under emergency, recruiting officers shouted imprecations at young men, bullying them into enlisting. Everywhere, northerners felt great disappointment. Only nine months earlier, Lee's army had invaded Maryland and been thrown back, and now, a second invasion threatened to undo all that had been accomplished. Although good news kept pouring in from other theaters of the war, the Eastern Theater looked lost. A New York City newspaper editor reflected, "It is a sad comment upon the conduct of the war up to the present time that we are once more under the menace of a rebel invasion; the enemy is still in force and threatening."

With the citizenry thus frightened, the Army of the Potomac finally took action. Four days of prodding from Lincoln and Halleck had failed to prompt Hooker, but now, at 10 p.m., June 15, with the news of Milroy's devastating retreat choking headlines, Hooker sheepishly recognized, "I now feel that invasion is [Lee's] settled purpose." The next day, the Army of the Potomac began to move. Hastily, the soldiers packed their belongings and struck their tents, struggling to make up for lost time. They needed to get over the Occoquan River and protect the western approaches into Washington, D.C. The marches on June 16 and 17 stretched the soldiers to the limits of endurance. On June 17, for instance, the 5th Corps trudged on for twelve hours, covering seventeen miles. The temperature reached the mid-90s and the corps lost a dozen men killed by heatstroke, including a popular regimental commander. The hard marching, combined with the news of the invasion, frustrated many. In fact, when the exhausted infantrymen made camp— apparently proud they had completed such a hard trek—Hooker surprised them by issuing a circular in which he expressed disappointment at their slow pace. Calling the circular unfair, a worn-out Vermont soldier wrote to his local paper, "General Hooker knows how to plan hard marching and hard fighting, but whether he knows enough to catch Gen. Lee remains to be seen."

For the next week, the two opposing armies marched north, roughly parallel to each other. On the Confederate side, Ewell's corps led the way, with Maj. Gen. Robert Rodes's division crossing the Potomac River at Williamsport, Maryland, on June 15. By June 22, Rodes's men were in Pennsylvania. Meanwhile, Longstreet's and Hill's corps followed behind at a greater distance. The last of Lee's infantry entered Pennsylvania on June 27.

As Lee's soldiers made their way into Pennsylvania, they made certain to partake of the splendors of a land untouched by war. Lee allowed his senior officers the authority to requisition supplies from the enemy populace

Lieut. Gen. Richard S. Ewell commanded the C.S. corps that routed the Union garrison at Winchester. Having recently elevated Ewell to corps command, Lee hoped that Ewell would demonstrate competence equal to his predecessor, Stonewall Jackson. The thrilling victory at Winchester seemed to suggest that Lee had made the correct choice; however, on July 1, at Gettysburg, Ewell's performance generated far more controversy. (Library of Congress)

Maj. Gen. Robert Milroy commanded the Union garrison at Winchester. Lincoln and his chief advisor, Maj. Gen. Henry Halleck, advised Milroy to abandon the city before Lee's army came within range; however, Milroy made an unwise decision to stay and fight. After Confederate troops overran one of his forts, Milroy ordered a belated retreat, which led to the capture of about 4,000 of his soldiers. (Library of Congress)

and seize them if they were not offered willingly. Under General Orders 72 (issued on June 21), the chiefs of the army's Ordnance, Commissary, Quartermaster, and Medical departments could make demands. Any Pennsylvanian who freely offered private property would receive "market price," but those who refused would have their property confiscated.

In execution, Confederate requisitions were excessive. For instance, at York, Maj. Gen. Jubal Early demanded $100,000 in U.S. currency. Additionally, he called for 2,000 pairs of shoes, 1,000 hats, 1,000 pairs of socks, and three days' worth of rations for his men. This far exceeded what the citizens of York had available to them. In the end, York provided only a portion of the requested footwear and headgear and only $28,600 of the ransom. Before leaving the city, Early required the leading businessmen to post a $50,000 bond to supply the remainder.

Despite Lee's plan to have his soldiers act compassionately when it came to requisitioning, his men, either individually or collectively, took whatever they pleased. One Pennsylvania farmer claimed the loss of 335 bushels of wheat, corn, and oats and twelve tons of hay, all taken by a Louisiana Brigade that encamped in his yard. A clothing business in York lost 912 articles (coats, hats, shirts, underwear, suspenders, pocket handkerchiefs, and socks) during the two-day rebel occupation of the city. When Col. Elijah V. White's cavalry battalion entered Gettysburg on June 26, his men stole horses, apparently with little compassion for those they robbed. One of White's troopers hauled off a horse owned by butcher James Pierce. Begging and weeping, Pierce's daughter, Tillie, pleaded with them to not to do it. One "impudent and coarse" trooper rejoined, "Sissy, what are you crying about? Go in the house and mind your own business." When James Pierce attempted to negotiate with Col. White about the horse, the Confederates turned him away, having heard he was an abolitionist. Apparently, a family of rival Democrats—the Wades—had already told the Confederates not to trust the Pierces because of their political proclivities. Eager to punish any Republicans, White's cavalry made certain that James Pierce would regret casting his vote in the Election of 1860.

Confederate soldiers did not destroy property wantonly, although there were a few notable exceptions. On June 26, Confederate infantry purposefully torched the Caledonia Iron Works because a Radical Republican Congressman, Thaddeus Stevens, owned it. Bitter at Stevens's support of confiscation and emancipation—two political issues that angered Confederate citizens—troops under Jubal Early put the foundry to the torch and seized all of Stevens's working animals. By Stevens's own reckoning, the destruction cost him about $75,000. In a dismissive tone, Stevens wrote, "If, finally, the government shall be reestablished over our whole territory; and not a vestige of slavery left, I shall deem it a cheap purchase."

Confederate soldiers also participated in brazen kidnappings of African Americans. During the invasion, Confederate officers assumed that black citizens living in lower Pennsylvania were runaways. As the gray-clad soldiers marched into Pennsylvania, some of them stole away from the column to abduct African Americans. Two Confederate units—Brig. Gen. John D. Imboden's and Brig. Gen. Albert Jenkins's brigades—perpetrated the bulk of the seizures. "They were on a regular slave-hunt," remembered a resident of Mercersburg who watched helplessly as soldiers from the 16th Virginia Cavalry snatched up his neighbors. According to him, these kidnappings "presented the worst spectacle I have yet seen in this war. They proclaimed, first, that they would burn down every house which harbored a fugitive slave and did not deliver him up in twenty minutes." Presently, no evidence yet catalogues the exact number of black Pennsylvanians kidnapped, but best estimates suggest that between fifty and 100 residents—men, women, and children—were abducted from Chambersburg, McConnellsburg, Mercersburg, and Greencastle.

During the advance, Lee followed no grand scheme, issuing instructions only as daily reconnaissance came to him. Much of Lee's reluctance to develop a plan came from the fact that his infantry vanguard—Ewell's corps—did not possess a strong cavalry force to screen its advance. At the outset of the campaign, Lee assigned one cavalry brigade—Brig. Gen. Albert Jenkins's—to assist Ewell's corps. As his army moved deeper into enemy territory, Lee elected to send three more cavalry brigades to Ewell, but these troops never reached him. On June 22, Lee advised his cavalry commander, Stuart, to leave two brigades to guard the gaps in the Blue Ridge Mountains, while Stuart took the other three into Maryland to link up with Ewell.

Specifically, Lee directed Stuart to connect with the right flank of Early's division, which was then crossing the Potomac River at Boteler's Ford. To accomplish this tricky maneuver, Lee suggested that Stuart detach his command, pass through the Loudoun Valley, and swing around behind the Army of the Potomac. After that, Stuart's men could cross into Maryland. One of Lee's corps commanders, Longstreet, offered Stuart the same advice, pointing out the necessity of getting the rebel horsemen behind the Union army so as not to disclose the movement of the infantry column. That same day, Longstreet wrote to Stuart, "You had better not leave us, therefore, unless you take the proposed route in rear of the enemy."

Unfortunately, the route proposed by Lee and Longstreet did not work as intended. Stuart moved his cavalry through Glasscock Gap and collided with Union troops—Maj. Gen. Winfield S. Hancock's 2nd Corps—near the village of Haymarket. After pulling back from this skirmish, Stuart made an unwise decision. Rather than backtrack into the Loudoun Valley, or even consult with Lee or Longstreet, he elected to continue farther south, and then father east, not at all following the path Lee or Longstreet had intended. Even today, Stuart's reasons for making such a radical departure are unclear. Most likely, Stuart assumed he could complete his mission—linking up with Ewell—even if he took this wider path. Also, on prior occasions, his cavalry had ridden around the Union army with impunity. Quite possibly, he did not doubt their ability to reprise their earlier performances. Strangely, Stuart did not believe the necessity of maintaining close connection with the infantry column superseded Lee's request to swing behind the Union army.

On the 26th, Stuart's three brigades left Buckland and made haste for the Occoquan River. The next day, they crossed into Maryland at Rowser's Ford. Their advance was delayed because it took hours to rig a bridge over the C. & O. Canal. Then, on June 28, Stuart unexpectedly diverted his column farther east toward Rockville, where he hoped to find badly needed forage for his horses. By happenstance, the Confederate cavalrymen stumbled upon a Union supply train and captured it, which Stuart celebrated as a signal victory. By this point, Stuart's

During the last week of June, Lee's cavalry commander, Maj. Gen. James E. B. Stuart, took three brigades on a needlessly long journey behind Union lines. Stuart's cavalrymen were unable to complete their primary mission, screening the vanguard of Lee's infantry. In the years following the Civil War, historians blamed Stuart for abandoning the Army of Northern Virginia in its hour of need. (Library of Congress)

command was well behind Hooker's army, and with the captured wagons in tow, he finally turned his command northward. He was more than ninety miles from his objective—the rendezvous with Early's division—and utterly useless to the rest of Confederate army because he could no longer provide it with crucial reconnaissance information.

Since 1863, historians have quibbled endlessly about who should bear the blame for Stuart's digression. Certainly, Lee and Longstreet gave Stuart poor advice. Additionally, the lackluster grazing compelled Stuart to move farther east than planned. But the decision to move so far out of the way must ultimately rest with Stuart himself. Maj. Henry B. McClellan of Stuart's staff later remarked, "Stuart's orders directed him to choose the most expeditious route by which to place himself on the right of Early's advance into Pennsylvania." Stuart chose this path of his own volition. That fact cannot be in doubt; but why he ignored one of the basic principles of cavalry operations may never be known. Wise or unwise, Stuart's decision shaped the path of Confederate movements and contributed to Lee's inability to understand the position of his foe.

As Lee's army gained ground in Pennsylvania, Hooker struggled with the War Department. Most of Hooker's correspondence went to Halleck, even though the two men despised each other. When news of the fall of Winchester became known, Hooker telegraphed Lincoln, hoping that he might restructure the chain of command so that he would not have to pass every decision through Halleck. Hooker argued that, so long as Halleck continued to hold a position in Washington as a chief military advisor to the President, "[W]e may look in vain for success." Hooker expected Lincoln to remove or admonish Halleck, but instead, the President clarified the relationship by giving Halleck's advice supremacy over Hooker's suggestions. On June 16, Lincoln telegraphed Hooker, "I shall direct him to give you orders and you to obey them."

Halleck did not make the awkward relationship any easier. For several days, he misled Hooker, advising him to move west to protect the federal garrison at Harpers Ferry and then admonishing him for making plans to move in that direction. Frustrated, Hooker orchestrated a power play designed to strip Halleck of his authority. He began requesting reinforcements, demanding authority over nearby units. At first, Halleck assented to this request. Since May, the Army of the Potomac had lost thirty-eight regiments, all of which had reached the end of their two-year tours-of-duty. With numbers dwindling, the army needed a new injection of manpower. Accordingly, Halleck reassigned five brigades to it from garrison duty and he gave Hooker authority to direct units in the Middle Department, the military subdivision that included Washington and Baltimore. But Hooker wanted more than that. On June 27, two days after crossing the Potomac River, he arrived at Harpers Ferry and demanded control of the garrison. From Washington, Halleck replied that Harpers Ferry could not be yielded. It held such strategic importance that it could not be abandoned unless absolutely necessary.

Hooker disagreed. He telegraphed Halleck, "Now they are but bait for the rebels, should they return." Fearing the garrison might be forced to surrender the same way as Milroy's men—and

From June 23, 1862, to March 12, 1864, Maj. Gen. Henry W. Halleck served as Lincoln's General-in-Chief, advising him from Washington, D.C. During the Gettysburg Campaign, Halleck became embroiled in an intense feud with Hooker. When the sniping between Hooker and Halleck could not be contained, Hooker offered his resignation, which Lincoln accepted. (Library of Congress) knowing the newspapers would undoubtedly blame him if such a disaster occurred—Hooker telegraphed an ultimatum. At 1 p.m., he informed Halleck that he must receive command of the Harpers Ferry garrison or he would tender his resignation. Believing he was under obligation to protect both Harpers Ferry and Washington, and that he could not consistently do both without authority over the former, Hooker telegraphed, "I am unable to comply with this condition with the means at my disposal, and earnestly request that I may at once be relieved from the position I occupy."

Hooker did not expect his threat of resignation would be taken seriously. Likely, he viewed it as a calculated ploy to rid himself of Halleck's oversight. However, Hooker underestimated Halleck's political cunning. Immediately, Halleck took Hooker's resignation to Lincoln, and advised him to accept it. The news of Hooker's resignation came as a shock to the President. He had no desire to relieve the commander of the Army of the Potomac while Confederate forces were raiding Pennsylvania. But Halleck pointed out the folly of abandoning Harpers Ferry, a crucial supply depot that guarded the confluence of the Potomac and Shenandoah rivers. Lincoln consulted with Secretary of War Edwin Stanton, who told him that, if Lincoln chose to replace Hooker, one of the army's corps commanders, Maj. Gen. George G. Meade, would make a suitable replacement.

With that advice in mind, Lincoln accepted Hooker's resignation and promptly dispatched an officer—Lieut. Col. James Hardie—to take an overnight train to Frederick, locate Meade, and inform him of his promotion. The next day, Lincoln informed the rest of his cabinet about Hooker's removal. One of them, Gideon Welles, recorded an opinion in his journal. Hooker, Welles wrote, possessed certain faults of character that could not be tolerated in the present crisis, namely, "want of alacrity to obey, and a greedy call for more troops which could not, and ought not to be taken from other points."

As the Union army underwent its change of command, the Confederates made a bold move to take the Pennsylvania capital. On June 28, still confident that the Army of the Potomac was south of the Potomac River, Lee sent orders to Ewell, instructing him to cross the Susquehanna River and begin an advance on Harrisburg. At that moment, Ewell was in Carlisle with one of his divisions. Another division—Jubal Early's—started the day at York, making haste for Wrightsville, where a covered bridge over one mile long spanned the Susquehanna. Early's men reached Wrightsville at about 5.30 p.m., but they found the bridge protected by 1,800 of Curtin's Emergency Militia, including a newly raised company of African Americans, the first of its kind from the state. Early's artillery unlimbered and commenced firing. Promptly, the Pennsylvania militia retreated across the bridge, setting fire to it as they ran. Early's infantry arrived too late to douse the flames. They formed a bucket brigade and worked all night, but by midnight, a great swath of the bridge was gone. Early expressed profound disappointment. As he later wrote, his plan to take Harrisburg was "entirely thwarted" by the destruction of the bridge. When Early turned in for the night, he expected he would have to map out a new route across the Susquehanna.

By morning, invading Harrisburg was no longer an option.

Maj. Gen. Joseph Hooker commanded the Army of the Potomac from January 26 to June 28, 1863. Prideful and ambitious, he became resentful when northern newspapers blamed him for the disaster at Chancellorsville. After the fall of Winchester, Hooker made several unreasonable demands on the U.S. War Department, threatening resignation if Lincoln did not reassign additional troops to Hooker's army. Unable to quell Hooker's bitterness, Lincoln accepted his resignation. (NARA)

OPPOSING COMMANDERS

At 3 a.m., June 28, on the grounds of Arcadia in Frederick, Maryland, Lieut. Col. James Hardie entered the tent of **Maj. Gen. George G. Meade**, the 5th Corps commander, and awakened him. Hardie joked that he had come to give Meade trouble. At first, Meade worried that Hardie had come to arrest him, a real possibility since Meade had criticized Hooker in some of his recent correspondence. Hardie joked that his mission was quite the contrary. He handed Meade a communication from Halleck, placing him in command of the Army of the Potomac. As Meade wrote to his wife, "As a soldier, I had nothing to do but accept and exert my utmost abilities to command success."

Meade read Halleck's message, which advised him to keep Washington and Baltimore protected at all hazards. If Lee's army turned toward either location, Halleck instructed, "[Y]ou will either anticipate him or arrive with him so as to give him battle." Without ado, Meade called Hooker to his tent, along with his chief of staff, Maj. Gen. Daniel Butterfield, and held an impromptu council of war. From Hooker, Meade learned the whereabouts of the rest of the army. Much of the army was scattered. The 1st, 3rd, 11th, and 12th corps were west of the Catoctin Mountains, all at different locations. The 2nd and 6th corps were farther south at Barnesville and Poolesville, respectively. At 7 a.m., Meade replied to Halleck, confessing ignorance to the enemy's strength and position, but he promised to advance his army toward the Susquehanna River and "give him battle."

Like many senior officers who survived the Civil War with an intact reputation, Meade was an unlikely choice to command an army. Cantankerous and hard to please, at age forty-seven, he had risen only as high as the rank of major in the regular army. He was born December 31, 1815, in Cádiz, Spain. Meade's father, a Philadelphia merchant, visited Spain during the Peninsular War, taking his family with him. Not long after Meade's birth, the family returned to the U.S., having lost hundreds of thousands of dollars due to unpaid debts from the Spanish monarchy. A few years after the untimely death of his father, Meade entered the U.S. Military Academy at West Point. In 1835, he graduated in the middle of his class and received a commission as second lieutenant in the 3rd U.S. Artillery. In 1840, he married Margaretta Sergeant, the daughter of a prominent Whig politician, and this marriage resulted in seven children. (In 1863, one of them, George G. Meade, Jr., served on his father's staff.) Prior to the war, Meade held several commands. In the 1840s, he served

During the early morning hours of June 28, 1863, a staff officer delivered news to Maj. Gen. George Meade's tent, telling him that he now commanded the Army of the Potomac. Although Meade did not witness any of the fighting during the first day of the battle, he monitored the situation closely from the army's Taneytown headquarters. (Library of Congress)

as a topographic engineer, supervising the construction of lighthouses and breakwaters along the Atlantic coast. During the war with Mexico, he served as a staff officer, earning distinction at the Battle of Palo Alto.

Meade began the Civil War at the rank of captain. However, with the implementation of the volunteer corps, Meade accepted a second substantive rank, that of brigadier general. In August 1861, he assumed command of a brigade assigned to the Pennsylvania Reserve Division. At the Battle of Glendale Crossroads, June 30, he was wounded in the forearm and hip. He recovered quickly, returned to command in August, and on September 12, 1862, received command of the division. He led it into the battles of South Mountain, Antietam, and Fredericksburg. By the end of September, the Senate confirmed his promotion to major general, and in the spring of 1863, he took command of the 5th Corps, leading it through the Chancellorsville Campaign.

During Joseph Hooker's tenure, Meade was fiercely critical of army leadership. Although he rarely shared his opinions publicly, Meade made his disappointment clear in letters to family and friends. After Chancellorsville, he wrote his wife, "Hooker has disappointed the army and myself in failing to show nerve … I am sorry for Hooker, because I like him and my relations have always been agreeable with him; but I cannot shut my eyes to the fact that he has on this occasion missed a brilliant opportunity."

Paranoid that his private opinions had leaked to the press, Meade worried that his days with the Army of the Potomac were numbered. But the opposite happened. On June 28, he received command of the Army of the Potomac and held it until the end of the war. Over the next few days, Meade familiarized himself with the army's gargantuan staff. By July 1, his headquarters made it only as far as Taneytown, Maryland. When the Battle of Gettysburg began, Meade monitored the situation from there, and for good reason, considering its location. It proved to be an ideal location from which to reorient his scattered corps. Consequently, Meade did not see any fighting on July 1.

Meade had been in command of the Army of the Potomac for only three days before the bloodiest battle of the Civil War began. His counterpart, **Robert E. Lee,** had been in command for much longer. Unlike Meade, Lee was well known and considered one of the brightest military minds on the continent. He was born on January 19, 1807, which made him fifty-six years old during the Battle of Gettysburg. He was the son of a famous Revolutionary War officer, Henry Lee III. After graduating near the top of his class at West Point, Lee received a commission as second lieutenant in the U.S. Army Corps of Engineers. In June 1831, he married Mary Anna Randolph Custis, the great-granddaughter of Martha Washington, a marriage that resulted in the birth of seven children, three of whom eventually served in the Confederate army. Like Meade, Lee also served in the war with Mexico, but on the staff of Gen. Winfield Scott. In 1859, Lee earned fame (or notoriety) for leading the operation that resulted in the capture of John Brown and his raiders. By 1861, he held the rank of colonel in the regular army.

The politics of disunion greatly concerned Lee, largely because he became a plantation manager only a few years prior to Lincoln's election. Upon the death of his father-in-law, Lee inherited Arlington House, a vast estate on the shores of the Potomac River. Throughout his life, Lee had a complicated relationship with matters pertaining to slavery and race, but when he assumed control of his wife's inheritance, he ran Arlington tightly and occasionally with brutality. Infamously, he ordered three runaways to be flogged, perhaps

Robert E. Lee's wartime papers contained no definitive explanation for why he chose to invade Pennsylvania. In a letter to the Secretary of War, he suggested that the Confederacy's best chance for independence would come only if its armies gave "all the encouragement" it could to the "rising Peace Party of the North." Lee is depicted here (seated), photographed on April 16, 1865. His son, Maj. Gen. Custis Lee, stands at left. One of his staff officers, Col. Walter H. Taylor, stands at right. (Library of Congress)

as many as thirty-nine times. When stories of Lee's cruelty appeared in several abolitionist newspapers, Lee became circumspect, deeply suspicious of a culture that dared to criticize the manner in which he managed his household.

Consistently, Lee considered slavery to be a necessary evil, a foolish institution imposed upon the South, but one that he would never willingly oppose. Perhaps his opinions on slavery also influenced his decision to quit the U.S. Army. As Lee explained it, he expected that Union victory would lead to only one result, reconstruction of the South under military guidance, which could only mean the collapse of the South's racial hierarchy. After contemplating that prospect, Lee believed he could not participate in any kind of military action against his home state. Perhaps with a tone of hyperbole, Lee predicted, "If … I remain on the side of the north, I must become a stranger in a strange land—far from the sod under which my ancestors lie buried. I can never again revisit the scenes of my childhood without meeting at every step the ghosts who may well say—we deserved better things at your hands."

Of course, Lee need not have been a stranger to the U.S. government, which adamantly desired his services. In April 1861, one of Lincoln's advisors, Francis P. Blair, offered Lee command of all U.S. forces being raised to subdue the rebellion. Lee refused, twice in fact. That same day, he held a meeting with his mentor, Winfield Scott, who repeated the offer. Again, Lee walked away from the opportunity. The nation had asked him to serve in a time of crisis and preserve the republic for which his own father had bled, but Lee's dedication to the U.S. Army came up short. It was a deeply emotional moment for Lee, and as he confessed, caused him great "mental agony."

Having severed his connection to the army, Lee offered his services to the rebellion. On June 14, 1861, he became a "full general" in the Confederate army. Despite the optimism that many Confederate citizens had about Lee's tactical acumen, he bungled his first Civil War campaign, which involved the defense of western Virginia. Over the first six months of the war, he demonstrated persistent timidity and yielded much of western Virginia to Union invasion. In fact, Confederate newspapers howled in protest when Lee kept receiving assignments. A legion of critics complained that Lee was too shy for combat. In 1862, the War Department finally reassigned him to Richmond, where he served as a military advisor to Jefferson Davis. Stationed far behind the lines, Lee's cautious approach, some believed, could not threaten the Confederacy's chances.

But then in June, the commander of the Army of Northern Virginia fell wounded at the Battle of Seven Pines. At Davis's request, Lee assumed command and he led that army with aplomb. For the next thirteen months, Lee fought aggressively, attacking Union troops with boldness and precision, winning engagements on the Peninsula, at Manassas, at Fredericksburg, and at Chancellorsville. Lee and his army often faced daunting odds, but he pulled off decisive victories that stunned the North. In a short amount of time, Lee's reputation made an abrupt turnaround. By 1863, many Confederate soldiers and citizens idolized him. Just days after defeating the Army of the Potomac on the Peninsula, the *Richmond Dispatch* concluded, "The rise which this officer has suddenly taken in the public confidence is without precedent." Undoubtedly, Lee's popularity reached its peak after Chancellorsville. Confidently, a South Carolinian who fought there wrote home: "Genl Lee says his infantry can never be whipped."

OPPOSING ARMIES

Heavy losses occurred on July 1 because the two opposing forces that clashed at Gettysburg consisted of combat-tested units filled with men who believed their nation's existence was staked in the battle's outcome. Although each army believed in oppositional values, both were equally willing to sacrifice life and limb to achieve victory.

The **Army of Northern Virginia** came into existence on April 6, 1862, with the passage of Special Order Number 6. That order consolidated several scattered commands from within the "Department of Northern Virginia" to create an army of the same name. Gen. Joseph E. Johnston assumed command, and after his wounding at the Battle of Seven Pines, Lee replaced him, holding command of the army until it surrendered in April 1865.

Although the Army of Northern Virginia did not exist *officially* until 1862, most soldiers who belonged to it had been in service since 1861. By Gettysburg, Lee's soldiers had compiled an impressive record, having fought at Big Bethel, Bull Run, Ball's Bluff, the Shenandoah Valley, the Peninsula Campaign, the 1862 Manassas Campaign, the Maryland Campaign, Fredericksburg, Chancellorsville, and the Siege of Suffolk. In June 1863, the Army of Northern Virginia numbered 70,226 officers and men. The soldiers were in high spirits and eager to invade Pennsylvania. A Georgian in Longstreet's corps spoke for many when he wrote home on June 26: "[W]e are now making the greatest movement of the war and will make Yankeedom howl and I hope to God, make them cry out 'Peace, peace.' … Our army is in good condition enjoying plenty to eat and wear and confident of success. Molly, I think this is the last year of the war, God grant it."

Four divisions of Confederate infantry experienced the bulk of the fighting on July 1: Maj. Gen. Henry Heth's, Maj. Gen. William D. Pender's, Maj. Gen. Robert E. Rodes's, and Maj. Gen. Jubal Early's. Pender's, Rodes's, and Early's divisions constituted three of the army's best units. All three had been in active service since 1862. Having experienced a near unbroken string of victories under Lee's command, these soldiers boasted high confidence. A lieutenant in Pender's division wrote, "I have little doubt now that we [have] now the finest army marshalled on this side of the Atlantic, and one scarcely inferior to any Europe has known … The victories of 1862 and the great battle of Chancellorsville this year [have] led us to believe scarcely anything impossible to Lee's army."

This photograph depicts two members of the 12th North Carolina Infantry, Pvt. Thomas D. Hilliard (left) and Corp. John Hilliard (right). The 12th North Carolina fought at Oak Ridge, losing 79 of its 219 officers and men. Both Hilliard brothers outlived the Battle of Gettysburg, but Thomas was killed at the Battle of Harris Farm, May 19, 1864. (Library of Congress)

In this image, Pvt. W. T. Harbison of the 11th North Carolina wears a six-button sack coat with black cloth epaulettes common among North Carolina regiments early in the war. By Gettysburg, these jackets were less common. At Gettysburg, the 11th North Carolina lost 366 out of 617 officers and men. Most of its casualties fell at the Herbst Woodlot. (Library of Congress)

Yet, some fractures existed. After the bloodbath at Chancellorsville, these three divisions lost heavily to desertion, particular in the ranks of the North Carolina brigades. In April, Pender complained to his wife that, "our N.C. soldiers are deserting very rapidly. I have had about 30 in the last 20 days." One of Pender's regiments counted 200 subtractions in the space of a month. The other division—Heth's—contained two brigades that, until recently, had been serving the Confederacy's backwaters. Likewise, these brigades struggled with desertion. Back in January 1863, in order to break its streak of deserters, Brig. Gen. J. J. Pettigrew's brigade formed up to witness the public execution of Pvt. Andrew Wyatt of the 26th North Carolina. In a surprise twist, during the ceremony, Wyatt received a reprieve at the last minute. He resumed his place in the ranks, and six months later, he was killed at Gettysburg.

The blue-clad soldiers were not much different. Officially, the **Army of the Potomac** came into being with the publication of General Orders Number 1, August 20, 1861. Cobbling together several divisions that had been rushed to the defense of Washington, Maj. Gen. George B. McClellan transformed the "Division of the Potomac" into an army of the same name. For the next year, McClellan's army was always in the headlines, largely because newspaper correspondents accompanied it, sending back daily updates to a news-hungry public. Over the course of the next year, the Army of the Potomac fought in some of the bloodiest campaigns of the war, clashing with Lee's legions on the Yorktown Peninsula and in Maryland. In November 1862, when McClellan's disdain with the War Department grew to toxic levels, Lincoln relieved him. His replacement, Maj. Gen. Ambrose Burnside, led the Army of the Potomac for two months until fallout from the disastrous Fredericksburg Campaign compelled him to resign. Hooker assumed command after that. He lasted longer, holding command for five months, resigning on June 28.

Prior to the Battle of Gettysburg, the Army of the Potomac numbered 93,534 men. It consisted of seven infantry corps, a cavalry corps, and an independent artillery reserve. Two of the infantry corps—the 1st and 11th—bore the brunt of the fighting on July 1. Both units had accumulated plenty of combat experience and were filled with U.S. Volunteers. Although a variety of emotions drove these Union soldiers to service, devotion to a republican form of government formed the crux of their motivation. On May 12, thirty-four officers and men from Company E, 142nd Pennsylvania, signed a resolution that condemned peace activism in the North. They sent this missive to their local newspaper to make it clear that the Army of the Potomac, as a whole, would accept nothing less than complete victory over the Confederacy. The Pennsylvanians proclaimed, "We are endeavoring to do our duty, by serving the Army of the Union, and shall not shirk from dangers of death in defence of our principles." This particular company lived up to its promise. By the end of July 1, over half of its number were killed or wounded.

Even in the 11th Corps, where German immigrants or sons of German immigrants constituted the bulk of the recruits, devotion to the republic fueled the rank and file's willingness to sacrifice. One German in the 11th Corps wrote to his parents back in the Grand Duchy of Oldenberg: "But even if I should die in the fight for freedom & the preservation of the Union of this, my adopted homeland, then you should not be too concerned, for many brave sons of the German fatherland have already died on the field of honor."

Like its counterpart, the Army of the Potomac also suffered from a recent string of desertions and tried to curb them with public executions. In fact, as it marched north in pursuit of the Confederate army, on June 12, the 1st Corps paused along the road to Deep Run to execute Pvt. John P. Woods, an Indiana soldier who had deserted twice within the previous six months. Woods died horribly, being only maimed by the first volley. A second burst of fire was required to end his life. Although almost no 1st Corps soldiers believed this public execution improved their personal courage, the message sent by Woods's death was not lost. Now was not the time for the Army of the Potomac to forsake its solemn duty.

Probably, very few Union soldiers needed to be told that essential truth. Of all the Union corps, the 11th marched north with the biggest chip on its shoulder. Over the course of May and June, northern newspapers had heaped excessive guilt upon this corps, blaming it for the recent defeat at Chancellorsville. Feeling ostracized by the press, few 11th Corps soldiers were willing to accept culpability for the army's ultimate failure. Indeed, they had skedaddled from a stunning rebel attack, but only because headquarters had put them in an indefensible position. "Some body is to blame for the repulse," wrote an 11th Corps captain to his mother and sisters, "and I can't blame the men for it, nor the commanders of Brigades or Divisions, but it will rest with some one higher in authority."

No matter their level of morale, the bulk of the Army of the Potomac was ready for a rematch. On the march to Pennsylvania, one regimental commander boasted to his fiancée, "The regiment will go out strong in health and cheerful in spirit, and determined always to sustain its glorious history."

The Army of the Potomac was ready to fight.

This image depicts a Union infantry regiment poised for the march. This is the 110th Pennsylvania, photographed on April 24, 1863, at Falmouth, Virginia. The 110th Pennsylvania belonged to 3rd Corps, which missed the fighting on July 1, but it fought heavily on July 2. Seen here, the 110th Pennsylvania depicts a typical Army of the Potomac regiment during the Gettysburg Campaign. (Library of Congress)

This photograph depicts Battery B, 2nd U.S. Light Artillery (in limbered formation), in July 1862. At Gettysburg, this artillery battery was commanded by Lieut. Edward Heaton. It missed the first day's fighting, but its sister-battery—Battery A—was involved in the opening skirmish. (Library of Congress)

ORDERS OF BATTLE

ARMY OF NORTHERN VIRGINIA

General Robert E. Lee
Escort
   39th Virginia Cavalry Battalion
   (two companies)
Imboden's Independent Command
   (Brig. Gen. John D. Imboden)
   18th Virginia Cavalry
   62nd Virginia Cavalry
   McNeill's Partisan Rangers
   (one company)
   Staunton Battery
Stuart's Cavalry Division
(Maj. Gen. James E. B. Stuart)
Hampton's Brigade
   (Brig. Gen. Wade Hampton)
   1st North Carolina Cavalry
   1st South Carolina Cavalry
   2nd South Carolina Cavalry
   Cobb's Legion Cavalry
   Jeff Davis Legion Cavalry
   Phillips's Legion Cavalry
Robertson's Brigade
   (Brig. Gen. Beverly H. Robertson)
   4th North Carolina Cavalry
   5th North Carolina Cavalry
Fitzhugh Lee's Brigade
   (Brig. Gen. Fitzhugh Lee)
   1st Maryland Cavalry Battalion
   1st Virginia Cavalry
   2nd Virginia Cavalry
   3rd Virginia Cavalry
   4th Virginia Cavalry
   5th Virginia Cavalry
Jenkins's Brigade
   (Brig. Gen. Albert G. Jenkins)
   14th Virginia Cavalry
   16th Virginia Cavalry
   17th Virginia Cavalry
   34th Virginia Cavalry Battalion
   36th Virginia Cavalry Battalion
   Jackson's Battery
William H. F. Lee's Brigade
   (Col. John R. Chambliss, Jr.)
   2nd North Carolina Cavalry
   9th Virginia Cavalry
   10th Virginia Cavalry
   13th Virginia Cavalry
Jones's Brigade (Brig. Gen. William E. Jones)
   6th Virginia Cavalry
   7th Virginia Cavalry
   11th Virginia Cavalry
Divisional Horse Artillery
   (Maj. Robert F. Beckham)
   Breathed's Battery
   Chew's Battery
   Griffin's Battery
   Hart's Battery
   McGregor's Battery
   Moorman's Battery

1ST CORPS

Lieut. Gen. James Longstreet
McLaws's Division
(Maj. Gen. Lafayette McLaws)
Kershaw's Brigade
   (Brig. Gen. Joseph B. Kershaw)
   2nd South Carolina Infantry
   3rd South Carolina Infantry
   7th South Carolina Infantry
   8th South Carolina Infantry
   15th South Carolina Infantry
   3rd South Carolina Battalion
Barksdale's Brigade
   (Brig. Gen. William Barksdale)
   13th Mississippi Infantry
   17th Mississippi Infantry
   18th Mississippi Infantry
   21st Mississippi Infantry
Semmes's Brigade
   (Brig. Gen. Paul J. Semmes)
   10th Georgia Infantry
   50th Georgia Infantry
   51st Georgia Infantry
   53rd Georgia Infantry
Wofford's Brigade
   (Brig. Gen. William T. Wofford)
   16th Georgia Infantry
   18th Georgia Infantry
   24th Georgia Infantry
   Cobb's Legion Infantry
   Phillips's Legion Infantry
   3rd Georgia Sharpshooter Battalion
Cabell's Artillery Battalion
   (Col. Henry C. Cabell)
   Battery A, 1st North Carolina Light
   Artillery
   Pulaski Artillery
   1st Richmond Howitzers
   Troup Artillery
Pickett's Division
(Maj. Gen. George E. Pickett)
Garnett's Brigade
   (Brig. Gen. Richard B. Garnett)
   8th Virginia Infantry
   18th Virginia Infantry
   19th Virginia Infantry
   28th Virginia Infantry
   56th Virginia Infantry
Kemper's Brigade (Brig. Gen. James L. Kemper)
   1st Virginia Infantry
   3rd Virginia Infantry
   7th Virginia Infantry
   11th Virginia Infantry
   24th Virginia Infantry
Armistead's Brigade (Brig. Gen. Lewis A.
   Armistead)
   9th Virginia Infantry
   14th Virginia Infantry
   38th Virginia Infantry
   53rd Virginia Infantry
   57th Virginia Infantry
Dearing's Artillery Battalion
   (Maj. James Dearing)
   Fauquier Artillery

Hampden Artillery
Richmond Fayette Artillery
Blount's Battery
Hood's Division (Maj. Gen. John B. Hood)
Law's Brigade (Brig. Gen. Evander M. Law)
   4th Alabama Infantry
   15th Alabama Infantry
   44th Alabama Infantry
   47th Alabama Infantry
   48th Alabama Infantry
Robertson's Brigade
   (Brig. Gen. Jerome B. Robertson)
   3rd Arkansas Infantry
   1st Texas Infantry
   4th Texas Infantry
   5th Texas Infantry
Anderson's Brigade
   (Brig. Gen. George T. Anderson)
   7th Georgia Infantry
   8th Georgia Infantry
   9th Georgia Infantry
   11th Georgia Infantry
   59th Georgia Infantry
Benning's Brigade
   (Brig. Gen. Henry L. Benning)
   2nd Georgia Infantry
   15th Georgia Infantry
   17th Georgia Infantry
   20th Georgia Infantry
Henry's Artillery Battalion
   (Maj. Mathias W. Henry)
   Branch Battery
   Charleston German Artillery
   Palmetto Light Artillery
   Rowan Artillery
Artillery Reserve (Col. James B. Walton)
Alexander's Artillery Battalion
   (Col. Edward P. Alexander)
   Ashland Artillery
   Bedford Artillery
   Brooks Artillery
   Madison Light Artillery
   Virginia (Richmond) Battery
   Virginia (Bath) Battery
Washington Artillery Battalion
   (Maj. Benjamin F. Eshleman)
   1st Company
   2nd Company
   3rd Company
   4th Company

2ND CORPS

Lieut. Gen. Richard S. Ewell
Provost Guard
   1st North Carolina Sharpshooter
   Battalion
Escort
   Randolph's Company, Virginia Cavalry
Early's Division (Maj. Gen. Jubal A. Early)
Hays's Brigade (Brig. Gen. Harry T. Hays)
   5th Louisiana Infantry
   6th Louisiana Infantry
   7th Louisiana Infantry
   8th Louisiana Infantry

9th Louisiana Infantry
Smith's Brigade (Brig. Gen. William Smith)
31st Virginia Infantry
49th Virginia Infantry
52nd Virginia Infantry
Hoke's Brigade (Col. Isaac E. Avery)
6th North Carolina Infantry
21st North Carolina Infantry
57th North Carolina Infantry
Gordon's Brigade (Brig. Gen. John B. Gordon)
13th Georgia Infantry
26th Georgia Infantry
31st Georgia Infantry
38th Georgia Infantry
60th Georgia Infantry
61st Georgia Infantry
Jones's Artillery Battalion
(Lieut. Col. Hilary P. Jones)
Charlottesville Artillery
Courtney Artillery
Louisiana Guard Artillery
Staunton Artillery
Cavalry
35th Virginia Cavalry Battalion

**Johnson's Division
(Maj. Gen. Edward Johnson)**
Steuart's Brigade (Brig. Gen. George H. Steuart)
1st Maryland Infantry Battalion
1st North Carolina Infantry
3rd North Carolina Infantry
10th Virginia Infantry
23rd Virginia Infantry
37th Virginia Infantry
Stonewall Brigade (Brig. Gen. James A. Walker)
2nd Virginia Infantry
4th Virginia Infantry
5th Virginia Infantry
27th Virginia Infantry
33rd Virginia Infantry
Nicholls's Brigade (Col. Jesse M. Williams)
1st Louisiana Infantry
2nd Louisiana Infantry
10th Louisiana Infantry
14th Louisiana Infantry
15th Louisiana Infantry
Jones's Brigade (Brig. Gen. John M. Jones)
21st Virginia Infantry
25th Virginia Infantry
42nd Virginia Infantry
44th Virginia Infantry
48th Virginia Infantry
50th Virginia Infantry
Andrews's Artillery Battalion
(Maj. Joseph W. Latimer)
1st Maryland Battery
Alleghany Artillery
Chesapeake Artillery
Lee Battery

Rodes's Division (Maj. Gen. Robert E. Rodes)
Daniel's Brigade (Brig. Gen. Junius Daniel)
32nd North Carolina Infantry
43rd North Carolina Infantry
45th North Carolina Infantry
53rd North Carolina Infantry
2nd North Carolina Infantry Battalion
Doles's Brigade (Brig. Gen. George P. Doles)
4th Georgia Infantry
12th Georgia Infantry
21st Georgia Infantry
44th Georgia Infantry

Iverson's Brigade (Brig. Gen. Alfred Iverson, Jr.)
5th North Carolina Infantry
12th North Carolina Infantry
20th North Carolina Infantry
23rd North Carolina Infantry
Ramseur's Brigade
(Brig. Gen. Stephen D. Ramseur)
2nd North Carolina Infantry
4th North Carolina Infantry
14th North Carolina Infantry
30th North Carolina Infantry
Rodes's Brigade (Col. Edward A. O'Neal)
3rd Alabama Infantry
5th Alabama Infantry
6th Alabama Infantry
12th Alabama Infantry
26th Alabama Infantry
Carter's Artillery Battalion
(Lieut. Col. Thomas H. Carter)
Jefferson Davis Artillery
King William Artillery
Morris Artillery
Orange Artillery

Artillery Reserve (Col. J. Thompson Brown)
First Virginia Artillery Battalion
(Capt. Willis J. Dance)
2nd Richmond Howitzers
3rd Richmond Howitzers
Powhatan Artillery
Rockbridge Artillery
Salem Artillery
Nelson's Artillery Battalion
(Lieut. Col. William Nelson)
Amherst Artillery
Fluvanna Artillery
Milledge's Georgia Battery

3RD CORPS

**Lieut. Gen. Ambrose P. Hill
Anderson's Division
(Maj. Gen. Richard H. Anderson)**
Wilcox's Brigade (Brig. Gen. Cadmus M. Wilcox)
8th Alabama Infantry
9th Alabama Infantry
10th Alabama Infantry
11th Alabama Infantry
14th Alabama Infantry
Mahone's Brigade (Brig. Gen. William Mahone)
6th Virginia Infantry
12th Virginia Infantry
16th Virginia Infantry
41st Virginia Infantry
61st Virginia Infantry
Wright's Brigade
(Brig. Gen. Ambrose R. Wright)
3rd Georgia Infantry
22nd Georgia Infantry
48th Georgia Infantry
2nd Georgia Infantry Battalion
Perry's Brigade (Col. David Lang)
2nd Florida Infantry
5th Florida Infantry
8th Florida Infantry
Posey's Brigade (Brig. Gen. Carnot Posey)
12th Mississippi Infantry
16th Infantry Mississippi Infantry
19th Mississippi Infantry
48th Mississippi
Cutts's Artillery Battalion (Maj. John Lane)
Company A

Company B
Company C
**Heth's Division (Maj. Gen. Henry Heth
[wounded on July 1]; Brig. Gen.
James J. Pettigrew)**
Pettigrew's Brigade
(Brig. Gen. James J. Pettigrew
[assumed divisional command on
July 1]; Col. James K. Marshall)
11th North Carolina Infantry
26th North Carolina Infantry
47th North Carolina Infantry
52nd North Carolina Infantry
Heth's Brigade (Col. John M. Brockenbrough)
40th Virginia Infantry
47th Virginia Infantry
55th Virginia Infantry
22nd Virginia Infantry Battalion
Archer's Brigade (Brig. Gen. James J. Archer
[captured on July 1]; Col. Birkett D. Fry)
13th Alabama Infantry
5th Alabama Infantry Battalion
1st Tennessee Infantry (1st Regiment,
C.S. Provisional Army)
7th Tennessee Infantry
14th Tennessee Infantry
Davis's Brigade (Brig. Gen. Joseph R. Davis)
2nd Mississippi Infantry
11th Mississippi Infantry
42nd Mississippi Infantry
55th North Carolina Infantry
Garnett's Artillery Battalion
(Lieut. Col. John J. Garnett)
Donaldsonville Artillery
Huger Artillery
Lewis Artillery
Norfolk Blues Artillery

**Pender's Division
(Maj. Gen. William D. Pender)**
McGowan's Brigade (Col. Abner M. Perrin)
1st South Carolina Infantry (1st
Regiment, C.S. Provisional Army)
1st South Carolina Rifles
12th South Carolina Infantry
13th South Carolina Infantry
14th South Carolina Infantry
Lane's Brigade (Brig. Gen. James H. Lane)
7th North Carolina Infantry
18th North Carolina Infantry
28th North Carolina Infantry
33rd North Carolina Infantry
37th North Carolina Infantry
Thomas's Brigade
(Brig. Gen. Edward L. Thomas)
14th Georgia Infantry
35th Georgia Infantry
45th Georgia Infantry
49th Georgia Infantry
Scales's Brigade
(Brig. Gen. Alfred M. Scales [wounded
on July 1]; Lieut. Col. George T. Gordon
[resumed regimental command on
July 1]; Col. William L. J. Lowrance)
13th North Carolina Infantry
16th North Carolina Infantry
22nd North Carolina Infantry
34th North Carolina Infantry
38th North Carolina Infantry

Poague's Artillery Battalion
(Maj. William T. Poague)
Albemarle Artillery
Charlotte Artillery
Madison Artillery
Brooke's Virginia Battery

Artillery Reserve (Col. Reuben L. Walker)
McIntosh's Artillery Battalion
(Maj. David G. McIntosh)
Danville Artillery
Hardaway Artillery
2nd Rockbridge Artillery
Johnson's Virginia Battery

Pegram's Artillery Battalion
(Maj. William R. J. Pegram)
Crenshaw Battery
Fredericksburg Artillery
Letcher Artillery
Pee Dee Artillery
Purcell Artillery

ARMY OF THE POTOMAC

Maj. Gen. George G. Meade
Provost Brigade
(Brig. Gen. Marsena R. Patrick)
93rd New York Infantry
8th United States Infantry
(eight companies)
2nd Pennsylvania Cavalry
6th Pennsylvania Cavalry
(two companies)
Escort
Oneida Cavalry (one company)
Engineer Brigade
(Brig. Gen. Henry W. Benham)
15th New York Engineers
(three companies)
50th New York Engineers
U.S. Engineer Battalion
**Artillery Reserve
(Brig. Gen. Robert O. Tyler)**
Headquarters Guard
32nd Massachusetts Infantry
(one company)
Train Guard
4th New Jersey Infantry
(seven companies)
1st Regular Brigade (Capt. Dunbar R. Ransom)
Battery H, 1st United States
Light Artillery
Batteries F and K, 3rd United
States Artillery
Battery C, 4th United States
Light Artillery
Battery C, 5th United States
Light Artillery
1st Volunteer Brigade
(Lieut. Col. Freeman McGilvery)
5th Massachusetts Light Artillery
and 10th New York Light Artillery
(consolidated)
9th Massachusetts Light Artillery
15th New York Light Artillery
Independent Batteries C and
F, Pennsylvania Light Artillery
(consolidated)
2nd Volunteer Brigade (Capt. Elijah D. Taft)
Battery B, 1st Connecticut
Heavy Artillery
Battery M, 1st Connecticut
Heavy Artillery
2nd Connecticut Light Artillery
5th New York Light Artillery
3rd Volunteer Brigade
(Capt. James F. Huntington)
1st New Hampshire Light Artillery
Battery H, 1st Ohio Light Artillery
Batteries F and G, 1st Pennsylvania
Light Artillery
Battery C, West Virginia Light Artillery
4th Volunteer Brigade
(Capt. Robert H. Fitzhugh)

6th Maine Light Artillery
Battery A, Maryland Light Artillery
1st New Jersey Light Artillery
Battery G, 1st New York Light Artillery
Battery K, 1st New York Light
Artillery and 11th New York Battery
(consolidated)

2ND CORPS

**Maj. Gen. Winfield S. Hancock
(assumed command of Left Wing
on the evening of July 1)
Brig. Gen. John Gibbon**
Headquarters Guard
Escort: 6th New York Cavalry
(two companies)
Provost Guard: 53rd Pennsylvania
Infantry (three companies)
Corps Artillery Brigade
(Capt. John G. Hazard)
Battery B, 1st New York Light Artillery
Battery A, 1st Rhode Island
Light Artillery
Battery B, 1st Rhode Island
Light Artillery
Battery I, 1st United States
Light Artillery
Battery A, 4th United States
Light Artillery
1st Division (Brig. Gen. John C. Caldwell)
1st Brigade (Col. Edward E. Cross)
5th New Hampshire Infantry
61st New York Infantry (four companies)
81st Pennsylvania Infantry
148th Pennsylvania Infantry
2nd Brigade (Col. Patrick Kelly)
28th Massachusetts Infantry
63rd New York Infantry
(two companies)
69th New York Infantry
(two companies)
88th New York Infantry
(two companies)
116th Pennsylvania Infantry
(four companies)
3rd Brigade (Brig. Gen. Samuel K. Zook)
52nd New York Infantry
57th New York Infantry
66th New York Infantry
140th Pennsylvania Infantry
4th Brigade (Col. John R. Brooke)
27th Connecticut Infantry
(two companies)
2nd Delaware Infantry
64th New York Infantry
53rd Pennsylvania Infantry
(seven companies)
145th Pennsylvania Infantry
(seven companies)

**2nd Division (Brig. Gen. John Gibbon
[assumed command of 2nd Corps on
evening of July 1]; Brig. Gen. William
Harrow)**
1st Company, Massachusetts Sharpshooters
1st Brigade (Brig. Gen. William Harrow
[assumed command of 2nd Division on
evening of July 1]; Col. Francis E. Heath)
19th Maine Infantry
15th Massachusetts Infantry
1st Minnesota Infantry
82nd New York Infantry (2nd New York
State Militia)
2nd Brigade (Brig. Gen. Alexander S. Webb)
69th Pennsylvania Infantry
71st Pennsylvania Infantry
72nd Pennsylvania Infantry
106th Pennsylvania Infantry
3rd Brigade (Col. Norman J. Hall)
19th Massachusetts Infantry
20th Massachusetts Infantry
7th Michigan Infantry
42nd New York Infantry
59th New York Infantry
(four companies)
3rd Division (Brig. Gen. Alexander Hays)
1st Brigade (Col. Samuel S. Carroll)
14th Indiana Infantry
4th Ohio Infantry
8th Ohio Infantry
7th West Virginia Infantry
2nd Brigade (Col. Thomas A. Smyth)
14th Connecticut Infantry
1st Delaware Infantry
12th New Jersey Infantry
10th New York Infantry
(four companies)
108th New York Infantry
3rd Brigade (Col. George L. Willard)
39th New York Infantry
(four companies)
111th New York Infantry
125th New York Infantry
126th New York Infantry

6TH CORPS

Maj. Gen. John Sedgwick
Headquarters Guard
1st New Jersey Cavalry (one company)
1st Pennsylvania Cavalry
(one company)
Artillery Brigade (Col. Charles H. Tompkins)
Battery A, 1st Massachusetts
Light Artillery
1st New York Light Artillery
3rd New York Light Artillery
Battery C, 1st Rhode Island
Light Artillery

Battery G, 1st Rhode Island
Light Artillery
Battery D, 2nd United States
Light Artillery
Battery G, 2nd United States
Light Artillery
Battery F, 5th United States
Light Artillery
1st Division (Brig. Gen. Horatio G. Wright)
Provost Guard
    4th New Jersey Infantry
    (three companies)
1st Brigade (Brig. Gen. Alfred T. A. Torbert)
    1st New Jersey Infantry
    2nd New Jersey Infantry
    3rd New Jersey Infantry
    15th New Jersey Infantry
2nd Brigade (Brig. Gen. Joseph J. Bartlett)
    5th Maine Infantry
    121st New York Infantry
    95th Pennsylvania Infantry
    96th Pennsylvania Infantry
3rd Brigade (Brig. Gen. David A. Russell)
    6th Maine Infantry
    49th Pennsylvania Infantry
    (four companies)
    119th Pennsylvania Infantry
    5th Wisconsin Infantry
2nd Division (Brig. Gen. Albion P. Howe)
2nd Brigade (Col. Lewis A. Grant)
    2nd Vermont Infantry
    3rd Vermont Infantry
    4th Vermont Infantry
    5th Vermont Infantry
    6th Vermont Infantry
3rd Brigade (Brig. Gen. Thomas H. Neill)
    7th Maine Infantry (six companies)
    33rd New York Infantry (one company)
    43rd New York Infantry
    49th New York Infantry
    77th New York Infantry
    61st Pennsylvania Infantry
3rd Division (Maj. Gen. John Newton)
1st Brigade (Brig. Gen. Alexander Shaler)
    65th New York Infantry

67th New York Infantry
122nd New York Infantry
23rd Pennsylvania Infantry
82nd Pennsylvania Infantry
2nd Brigade (Col. Henry L. Eustis)
    7th Massachusetts Infantry
    10th Massachusetts Infantry
    37th Massachusetts Infantry
    2nd Rhode Island Infantry
3rd Brigade (Brig. Gen. Frank Wheaton)
    62nd New York Infantry
    93rd Pennsylvania Infantry
    98th Pennsylvania Infantry
    139th Pennsylvania Infantry

CAVALRY CORPS

Maj. Gen. Alfred Pleasonton
1st Brigade, Horse Artillery
    (Capt. James M. Robertson)
    9th Michigan Battery
    6th New York Battery
    Batteries B and L, 2nd United States
    Light Artillery
    Battery M, 2nd United States
    Light Artillery
    Battery E, 4th United States
    Light Artillery
2nd Brigade, Horse Artillery
    (Capt. John C. Tidball)
    Batteries E and G, 1st United States
    Light Artillery
    Battery K, 1st United States
    Light Artillery
    Battery A, 2nd United States
    Light Artillery
1st Division (Brig. Gen. John Buford)
1st Brigade (Col. William Gamble)
    8th Illinois Cavalry
    12th Illinois Cavalry (four companies)
    3rd Indiana Cavalry (six companies)
    8th New York Cavalry
2nd Brigade (Col. Thomas Devin)
    6th New York Cavalry (six companies)
    9th New York Cavalry

17th Pennsylvania Cavalry
3rd West Virginia Cavalry
(two companies)
Reserve Brigade (Brig. Gen. Wesley Merritt)
    6th Pennsylvania Cavalry
    1st United States Cavalry
    2nd United States Cavalry
    5th United States Cavalry
    6th United States Cavalry
2nd Division
(Brig. Gen. David McM. Gregg)
Headquarters Guard
    1st Ohio Cavalry (one company)
1st Brigade (Col. John B. McIntosh)
    1st Maryland Cavalry
    (eleven companies)
    Purnell Legion Cavalry (one company)
    1st Massachusetts Cavalry
    1st New Jersey Cavalry
    1st Pennsylvania Cavalry
    3rd Pennsylvania Cavalry
    Battery H, 3rd Pennsylvania Heavy
    Artillery (one section, operating as
    light artillery)
3rd Brigade (Col. John I. Gregg)
    1st Maine Cavalry (ten companies)
    10th New York Cavalry
    4th Pennsylvania Cavalry
    16th Pennsylvania Cavalry
3rd Division
(Brig. Gen. H. Judson Kilpatrick)
Headquarters Guard
    1st Ohio Cavalry (one company)
1st Brigade (Brig. Gen. Elon J. Farnsworth)
    5th New York Cavalry
    18th Pennsylvania Cavalry
    1st Vermont Cavalry
    1st West Virginia Cavalry
    (ten companies)
2nd Brigade (Brig. Gen. George A. Custer)
    1st Michigan Cavalry
    5th Michigan Cavalry
    6th Michigan Cavalry
    7th Michigan Cavalry (ten companies)

LEFT WING ARMY OF THE POTOMAC (1ST, 3RD, AND 11TH CORPS)

Maj. Gen. John F. Reynolds
    (killed on July 1)
Maj. Gen. Abner Doubleday
    (resumed command of 1st Corps)
Maj. Gen. Oliver O. Howard
    (resumed command of 11th Corps)
Maj. Gen. Winfield S. Hancock

1ST CORPS

Maj. Gen. Abner Doubleday
Headquarters Guard
    1st Maine Cavalry (one company)
Corps Artillery Brigade
    (Col. Charles S. Wainwright)
    Battery B, 2nd Maine Light Artillery
    Battery E, 5th Maine Light Artillery
    Batteries E and L, 1st New York
    Light Artillery
    Battery B, 1st Pennsylvania Light Artillery
    Battery B, 4th United States
    Light Artillery

1st Division (Brig. Gen. James S. Wadsworth)
1st Brigade (Brig. Gen. Solomon Meredith
    [wounded on July 1];
    Col. William W. Robinson)
    19th Indiana Infantry
    24th Michigan Infantry
    2nd Wisconsin Infantry
    6th Wisconsin Infantry
    7th Wisconsin Infantry
2nd Brigade (Brig. Gen. Lysander Cutler)
    7th Indiana Infantry
    76th New York Infantry
    84th New York Infantry
    (14th Brooklyn Militia)
    95th New York Infantry
    147th New York Infantry
    56th Pennsylvania Infantry
    (nine companies)

2nd Division
(Brig. Gen. John C. Robinson)
1st Brigade (Brig. Gen. Gabriel R. Paul
    [wounded on July 1]; Col. Samuel H.
    Leonard [wounded on July 1]; Col.
    Adrian R. Root [wounded and captured
    on July 1]; Col. Richard Coulter)
    16th Maine Infantry
    13th Massachusetts Infantry
    94th New York Infantry
    104th New York Infantry
    107th Pennsylvania Infantry
2nd Brigade (Brig. Gen. Henry Baxter)
    12th Massachusetts Infantry
    83rd New York Infantry
    (9th New York State Militia)
    97th New York Infantry
    11th Pennsylvania Infantry
    88th Pennsylvania Infantry
    90th Pennsylvania Infantry

3rd Division
(Brig. Gen. Thomas A. Rowley)
1st Brigade (Col. Chapman Biddle)
  80th New York Infantry
  (20th New York State Militia)
  121st Pennsylvania Infantry
  142nd Pennsylvania Infantry
  151st Pennsylvania Infantry
2nd Brigade (Col. Roy Stone wounded
  on July 1]; Col. Langhorne Wister
  [wounded on July 1];
  Col Edmund L. Dana)
  143rd Pennsylvania Infantry
  149th Pennsylvania Infantry
  150th Pennsylvania Infantry
3rd Brigade (Brig. Gen. George J. Stannard)
  13th Vermont Infantry
  14th Vermont Infantry
  16th Vermont Infantry

3RD CORPS

Maj. Gen. Daniel E. Sickles
Corps Artillery Brigade
  (Capt. George E. Randolph)
  Battery B, 1st New Jersey Light Artillery
  Battery D, 1st New York Light Artillery
  4th New York Light Artillery
  Battery E, 1st Rhode Island
  Light Artillery
  Battery K, 4th United States Artillery
1st Division (Maj. Gen. David B. Birney)
1st Brigade (Brig. Gen. Charles K. Graham)
  57th Pennsylvania (eight companies)
  63rd Pennsylvania Infantry
  68th Pennsylvania Infantry
  105th Pennsylvania Infantry
  114th Pennsylvania Infantry
  141st Pennsylvania Infantry
2nd Brigade (Brig. Gen. J. H. Hobart Ward)
  20th Indiana Infantry
  3rd Maine Infantry
  4th Maine Infantry
  86th New York Infantry
  124th New York Infantry
  99th Pennsylvania Infantry
  1st United States Sharpshooters
  2nd United States Sharpshooters
  (eight companies)

3rd Brigade (Col. P. Régis D. d'K. de Trobriand)
  17th Maine Infantry
  3rd Michigan Infantry
  5th Michigan Infantry
  40th New York Infantry
  110th Pennsylvania Infantry
  (six companies)
2nd Division
(Brig. Gen. Andrew A. Humphreys)
1st Brigade (Brig. Gen. Joseph B. Carr)
  1st Massachusetts Infantry
  11th Massachusetts Infantry
  16th Massachusetts Infantry
  12th New Hampshire Infantry
  11th New Jersey Infantry
  26th Pennsylvania Infantry
2nd Brigade (Col. William R. Brewster)
  70th New York Infantry (1st Excelsior)
  71st New York Infantry (2nd Excelsior)
  72nd New York Infantry (3rd Excelsior)
  73rd New York Infantry (4th Excelsior)
  74th New York Infantry (5th Excelsior)
  120th New York Infantry
3rd Brigade (Col. George C. Burling)
  2nd New Hampshire Infantry
  5th New Jersey Infantry
  6th New Jersey Infantry
  7th New Jersey Infantry
  8th New Jersey Infantry
  115th Pennsylvania Infantry

11TH CORPS

**Maj. Gen. Oliver O. Howard (assumed
  command of Left Wing on afternoon
  of July 1)**
**Maj. Gen. Carl Schurz (resumed command
  of 3rd Division on evening of July 1)**
Maj. Gen. Oliver Howard
Headquarters Guard
  1st Indiana Cavalry (two companies)
  8th New York Infantry (one company)
Artillery Brigade (Maj. Thomas W. Osborn)
  Battery I, 1st New York Light Artillery
  13th New York Light Artillery
  Battery I, 1st Ohio Light Artillery
  Battery K, 1st Ohio Light Artillery
  Battery G, 4th United States
  Light Artillery

**1st Division (Brig. Gen. Francis C. Barlow
  [wounded and captured on July 1];
  Brig. Gen. Adelbert Ames)**
1st Brigade (Col. Leopold von Gilsa)
  41st New York Infantry
  (nine companies)
  54th New York Infantry
  68th New York Infantry
  153rd Pennsylvania Infantry
2nd Brigade (Brig. Gen. Adelbert Ames
  [assumed divisional command on
  July 1]; Col. Andrew L. Harris)
  17th Connecticut Infantry
  25th Ohio Infantry
  75th Ohio Infantry
  107th Ohio Infantry
2nd Division
(Brig. Gen. Adolph von Steinwehr)
1st Brigade (Col. Charles R. Coster)
  134th New York Infantry
  154th New York Infantry
  27th Pennsylvania Infantry
  73rd Pennsylvania Infantry
2nd Brigade (Col. Orland Smith)
  33rd Massachusetts Infantry
  136th New York Infantry
  55th Ohio Infantry
  73rd Ohio Infantry
**3rd Division (Maj. Gen. Carl Schurz
  [assumed command of 11th Corps on
  July 1]; Brig. Gen. Alexander
  Schimmelfennig [missing in action on
  evening of July 1]; Maj. Gen. Carl Schurz)**
1st Brigade (Brig. Gen. Alexander
  Schimmelfennig [assumed
  command of 3rd Division on July 1];
  Col. George von Amsberg)
  82nd Illinois Infantry
  45th New York Infantry
  157th New York Infantry
  61st Ohio Infantry
  74th Pennsylvania Infantry
2nd Brigade (Col. Włodzimierz
  Krzyżanowski)
  58th New York Infantry
  119th New York Infantry
  82nd Ohio Infantry
  75th Pennsylvania Infantry
  26th Wisconsin Infantry

RIGHT WING OF THE ARMY OF THE POTOMAC (5TH AND 12TH CORPS)
Maj. Gen. Henry W. Slocum

5TH CORPS

Maj. Gen. George Sykes
Headquarters Guard
  12th New York Infantry
  (two companies)
  17th Pennsylvania Cavalry
  (two companies)
Artillery Brigade (Capt. Augustus P. Martin)
  3rd Massachusetts Light Artillery
  Battery C, 1st New York Light Artillery
  Battery L, 1st Ohio Light Artillery
  Battery D, 5th United States
  Light Artillery
  Battery I, 5th United States
  Light Artillery

1st Division (Brig. Gen. James Barnes)
1st Brigade (Col. William S. Tilton)
  18th Massachusetts Infantry
  22nd Massachusetts Infantry
  2nd Company, Massachusetts
  Sharpshooters
  1st Michigan Infantry
  118th Pennsylvania Infantry
2nd Brigade (Col. Jacob B. Sweitzer)
  9th Massachusetts Infantry
  32nd Massachusetts Infantry
  (nine companies)
  4th Michigan Infantry
  62nd Pennsylvania Infantry
3rd Brigade (Col. Strong Vincent)
  20th Maine Infantry
  16th Michigan Infantry
  44th New York Infantry
  83rd Pennsylvania Infantry

2nd Division (Brig. Gen. Romeyn B. Ayres)
1st Brigade (Col. Hannibal Day)
  3rd United States Infantry
  (six companies)
  4th United States Infantry
  (four companies)
  6th United States Infantry
  (five companies)
  12th United States Infantry
  (eight companies)
  14th United States Infantry
  (eight companies)
2nd Brigade (Col. Sidney Burbank)
  2nd United States Infantry
  (six companies)
  7th United States Infantry
  (four companies)
  10th United States Infantry
  (three companies)

11th United States Infantry
(six companies)
17th United States Infantry
(seven companies)
3rd Brigade (Brig. Gen. Stephen H. Weed)
140th New York Infantry
146th New York Infantry
91st Pennsylvania Infantry
155th Pennsylvania Infantry
3rd Division
(Brig. Gen. Samuel W. Crawford)
1st Brigade (Col. William McCandless)
1st Pennsylvania Reserve Infantry
(nine companies)
2nd Pennsylvania Reserve Infantry
6th Pennsylvania Reserve Infantry
13th Pennsylvania Reserve Infantry
(1st Pennsylvania Rifles)
3rd Brigade (Col. Joseph W. Fisher)
5th Pennsylvania Reserve Infantry
9th Pennsylvania Reserve Infantry
10th Pennsylvania Reserve Infantry
11th Pennsylvania Reserve Infantry
12th Pennsylvania Reserve Infantry
(nine companies)

12TH CORPS

Maj. Gen. Henry W. Slocum (assumed command of Right Wing on July 1; Brig. Gen. Alpheus S. Williams)
Provost Guard: 10th Maine Infantry Battalion
(three companies)
Artillery Brigade
(Lieut. Edward D. Muhlenberg)
Battery M, 1st New York Light Artillery
Independent Battery E, Pennsylvania
Light Artillery
Battery F, 4th United States
Light Artillery
Battery K, 5th United States
Light Artillery
1st Division (Brig. Gen. Alpheus S. Williams [assumed command of 12th Corps on July 1]; Brig. Gen. Thomas H. Ruger)
1st Brigade (Col. Archibald L. McDougall)
5th Connecticut Infantry
20th Connecticut Infantry
3rd Maryland Infantry
123rd New York Infantry
145th New York Infantry
46th Pennsylvania Infantry
2nd Brigade (assigned as 2nd Brigade upon arrival, July 2; Brig. Henry H. Lockwood)
1st Maryland, Potomac Home Brigade
Infantry

1st Maryland, Eastern Shore Infantry
150th New York Infantry
3rd Brigade (Brig. Gen. Thomas H. Ruger [assumed command of 1st Division on July 1]; Col. Silas Colgrove)
27th Indiana Infantry
2nd Massachusetts Infantry
13th New Jersey Infantry
107th New York Infantry
3rd Wisconsin Infantry
2nd Division (Brig. Gen. John W. Geary)
1st Brigade (Col. Charles Candy)
5th Ohio Infantry
7th Ohio Infantry
29th Ohio Infantry
66th Ohio Infantry
28th Pennsylvania Infantry
147th Pennsylvania Infantry
(eight companies)
2nd Brigade (Col. George A. Cobham, Jr.)
29th Pennsylvania Infantry
109th Pennsylvania Infantry
111th Pennsylvania Infantry
3rd Brigade (Brig. Gen. George S. Greene)
60th New York Infantry
78th New York Infantry
102nd New York Infantry
137th New York Infantry
149th New York Infantry

This photograph depicts an unidentified soldier attached to the 14th Brooklyn Chasseurs (officially designated the 84th New York Infantry). Informally known as the "Brooklyn Zouaves," this regiment wore a distinctive uniform, complete with red trousers, white canvas leggings, and a red-trimmed shell jacket. The 14th Brooklyn participated in the morning clash, assisting in the repulse and capture of Confederate units near the middle railroad cut. On July 2 and 3, the 14th Brooklyn became involved in the fighting on Culp's Hill. It was one of the only Union regiments to endure heavy combat on all three days of the battle. The 14th Brooklyn took 318 officers and men into the battle and it lost 217 of them. (Library of Congress)

OPPOSING PLANS

During the last two weeks of June, the Army of Northern Virginia's invasion resembled a giant raid, but Lee was eager to change its tone. Anticipating the lure of a decisive battle, he thought hopefully about his army's next combat encounter. On the afternoon of June 27, Lee consulted with one of his generals, Maj. Gen. Isaac Trimble, who had been a civil engineer in Maryland prior to the war. Unfolding a map of Pennsylvania, Lee asked him about the topography of Adams County, Pennsylvania. Unprompted, Lee told Trimble about his plan to engage the Yankees as they crossed the Mason-Dixon Line:

> They will come up, probably through Frederick; broken down with hunger and hard marching, strung out on a long line and much demoralized, when they come into Pennsylvania. I shall throw an overwhelming force on their advance, crush it, follow up the success, drive one corps back on another, and by successive repulses and surprises before they can concentrate; create a panic and virtually destroy the army.

According to Trimble, Lee laid his hands on the map, waved them over Adams County (which included Gettysburg) and said, "We shall probably meet the enemy and fight a great battle, and if God gives us a victory, the war will be over and we shall achieve the recognition of our independence."

Lee envisioned a climactic battle to decide the fate of the rebellion, but that battle came sooner than he expected. On the evening of June 28, important news reached his headquarters. The Army of the Potomac had entered Frederick, Maryland. In a mere forty-eight hours, it would be in Pennsylvania. This news came as a shock, in part because it came from an unlikely source, a scout hired by James Longstreet. It vexed Lee to learn that such crucial reconnaissance information did not come from Stuart's cavalry. As Lee later explained, "It was expected that as soon as the Federal Army should cross the Potomac, General Stuart would give notice of its movements."

Having heard nothing from Stuart for the past week, Lee had inferred that the Army of the Potomac was still in Virginia. Now, with news to the contrary, Lee abruptly altered his army's plans to begin the consolidation scheme he had revealed to Trimble only the day before. That evening, Lee fired off two messages to Ewell, instructing him to abort his mission to the Susquehanna River and rejoin the main body of the army. Specifically, he directed Ewell to concentrate his corps at Heidlersburg and then rendezvous with the rest of the army at either Cashtown or Gettysburg, "as the circumstances might require."

Although deeply disappointed at being denied a chance to raid Pennsylvania's capital, Ewell dutifully made arrangements so that two of his divisions—Rodes's and Early's—could travel in the direction of both Cashtown and Gettysburg. If and when Lee decided, Ewell could send both divisions toward either destination without losing time.

Meanwhile, the Army of the Potomac's new commander, Meade, formulated his own plans. He proposed to send three corps—the 1st, 3rd, and 11th Corps—up through Emmitsburg, Maryland, while the rest would assemble at Frederick to then advance north and northeast of the city. Together, the entirety of the army would march to Pipe Creek, a tributary of the Monocacy River, which flowed into the Potomac south of Frederick. On the night of June 30, after a reconnaissance of Pipe Creek, Meade fashioned a plan, which involved a tactical defense. Meade's staff completed an army-wide circular, now known as the Pipe Creek Circular, which explained the army's coming movements. Meade wanted his infantry corps to take up defensive positions between two Maryland towns, Middleburg and Manchester, holding the line of Pipe Creek. Should Lee have decided to move his army in the direction of Baltimore or Washington, the Army of the Potomac would be well deployed, with all major roads covered and a strong line of supply in its rear.

However, Meade's plan fell apart because the army's "Left Wing"—the three corps at Emmitsburg—drifted too close to Lee's assembly point at Gettysburg. Maj. Gen. John F. Reynolds commanded the Left Wing. (Under normal circumstances, he commanded the 1st Corps, but as temporary wing commander, he relinquished command of the 1st Corps to his senior divisional commander, Maj. Gen. Abner Doubleday.) Before Meade drafted the Pipe Creek Circular on the 30th, he issued orders to Reynolds to advance to Gettysburg. At the time, Reynolds was headquartered at the village of Marsh Creek, two miles north of the Mason-Dixon Line. So far as Reynolds knew, if he chose Gettysburg as a place to give battle, he expected that Meade would support him with the rest of the army.

Meade's orders to take the Left Wing to Gettysburg may not have been necessary. Reynolds insisted on moving to Gettysburg when he discovered that another unit, the 1st Division, Cavalry Corps, had preceded him there. In his reports, the divisional commander, Brig. Gen. John Buford, never gave a specific reason for *his* decision to enter Gettysburg, but since his division had been serving as the army's advance reconnaissance unit, covering the army's left-front, moving to Gettysburg was the ideal way to execute his mission. From Gettysburg, Buford's troopers could gather crucial information by

Maj. Gen. John F. Reynolds commanded the Army of the Potomac's Left Wing. On the evening of June 30, he received Buford's message and decided to advance his three corps in the direction of Gettysburg. By bringing his infantry to the scene, Reynolds determined that the engagement would be more than a mere skirmish. After only a few minutes of being on the field, Reynolds was killed by a rifle ball to the head. (Library of Congress)

Brig. Gen. John Buford commanded a division of Union cavalry. On June 30, his troops entered Gettysburg and formed a vidette screen west and north of the borough. After discovering approaching Confederate infantry, Buford sent messages to nearby Union infantry commanders, alerting them of the danger. Buford's cavalrymen saw heavy action during July 1. They skirmished with Confederate soldiers for several hours in the morning, and in the afternoon, they held off the advance of a brigade of infantry. (NARA)

interviewing residents who had seen Confederates pass through the borough on June 26. Additionally, Buford's soldiers required feed for their horses, who were worn out from the balmy weather. He supposed that Gettysburg would be able to provide that relief.

It was a tough ride into the town. Buford's horsemen had been on the road since prior to dawn. Having found their way blocked through Fairfield by Confederate infantry, Buford's 2,700 troopers rerouted through Emmitsburg. By 11 a.m., June 30, they trotted into Gettysburg, having traveled more than twenty miles. Grateful citizens crowded the streets, singing songs and handing out bouquets. They gave Buford the information he expected, reporting that Early's infantry had been there four days ago and that another Confederate brigade—Pettigrew's—had approached earlier that morning, but had stopped short of the town.

Accompanied by one brigade and his headquarters staff, Buford passed through the town and turned left, exiting via the Chambersburg Pike. On the west side of town, he examined the ground carefully. Three major roads ran out of Gettysburg: the Mummasburg Road (which ran northwest), the Fairfield Road (which ran southwest), and the Chambersburg Pike (which ran west-northwest). (Of the three, the Chambersburg Pike was the widest and the most likely route from which Confederates might approach.) Also, an unfinished railroad bed ran along the north side of the pike, sporting three massive cuts where the grade barged through the rolling countryside. Several ridges, running north to south, undulated away from the town. Seminary Ridge—with a prominent divinity school atop it—sat at the outskirts of the borough. Beyond that was a ridge named for a local politician—McPherson's Ridge. One mile beyond that was Herr's Ridge (named for a nearby tavern), and one and half miles further still was Wisler's Ridge (named for a blacksmith shop).

Since this terrain admirably suited the needs of his cavalry, Buford dispersed his command along the three outermost ridges. He deployed a line of videttes—five-person outposts with an officer in charge—for seven miles, holding the region between the Mummasburg and Fairfield roads. An additional line of videttes from Buford's other brigade held positions north of town watching the Carlisle and Heidlersburg roads. Behind the line of videttes, two lines of skirmishers deployed dismounted, one line atop Herr's Ridge (about 200 troopers) and the other atop McPherson's Ridge. Buford dispersed his "horse artillery"—six light artillery pieces—along the pike to enhance the final line of defense, two sections near the McPherson farm and a third section 500 yards south of the John Herbst Woodlot. Buford made these dispositions because they enabled his troopers to gather information from several directions at once. Inadvertently, he had selected the battleground for the first day of the Battle of Gettysburg.

Buford's troopers kept him up to date on the known positions of the enemy. Four miles down the Chambersburg Pike, his scouts encountered a brigade of North Carolinians under Brig. Gen. J. Johnston Pettigrew. At that moment, Pettigrew's men were on a foraging expedition, and in the late afternoon, they caught sight of Buford's troopers shadowing them near Wisler's Ridge. His men kept the Union cavalrymen at a distance and Pettigrew reported the news to his divisional commander, Maj. Gen. Henry Heth, who was headquartered at Cashtown.

As Pettigrew and Heth tried to make heads or tails of Buford's scouts, the corps commander, Lieut. Gen. A. P. Hill, arrived on the scene. Together, the three men held an unplanned conference. Pettigrew stated his belief that the Union cavalry belonged to the Army of the Potomac, but the senior generals believed the unwelcomed guests belonged to Curtin's Emergency Militia. Hill expressed his opinion that the Army of the Potomac could not be as close as Gettysburg; therefore, the nearby enemy soldiers must be militia.

Feeling confident, Heth offered to take them on. As he remembered it, Heth announced his intention to advance toward Gettysburg the next day, July 1. Then, recognizing Hill's presence, he asked courteously, "Do you have any objection?" Hill replied, "None in the world." Neither Hill nor Heth mentioned the prospect of starting a battle, but both generals understood that advancing against the Union soldiers atop Wisler's Ridge—whoever they may be—would, in fact, commence an engagement. Hill left no account of the meeting, but in his action report, he explained that the decision to send forces into Gettysburg rested with him. He wrote, "I intended to advance the next morning and discover what was in my front."

Lieut. Gen. A. P. Hill commanded the Army of Northern Virginia's 3rd Corps. Although Lee had issued orders not to bring upon a general engagement until the army was concentrated, Hill authorized Heth's reconnaissance toward Gettysburg. After Heth's defeat on the fields west of Gettysburg, Hill elected to feed reinforcements into the fight. (Library of Congress)

In the years since the battle, historians have insisted that Hill violated a prime directive issued by Lee, not to bring about a general engagement until the army was concentrated. However, Hill's actions were not entirely out of line with the army's immediate mission. Lee required a location to concentrate his army and Gettysburg was the best choice. Although Hill could have elected to await the arrival of Ewell's men at Cashtown, he decided it would be best if his corps assembled with Ewell at Gettysburg. What Hill did not contemplate was the possibility that Union forces might frustrate this rendezvous. Dismissive of the potential danger, Hill (and to a lesser degree, Heth) made it inevitable that Gettysburg would be the site of a battle, even if they could not have predicted its size and ramifications.

The encounter between Pettigrew and Buford was not the only unintended action on June 30. Fourteen miles east of Gettysburg, Union and Confederate cavalry clashed along the southern outskirts of Hanover. Ever since his departure from the Confederate column on June 25, J. E. B. Stuart had been attempting to link up with Early's division, which he expected

33

to find at York. (Unbeknownst to him, Early's division was actually at Heidlersburg, twenty-two miles to the west.) Stuart's brigades had just come up from Maryland and attempted to pass through Hanover to make their belated rendezvous. Just prior to noon, Stuart's vanguard—the brigade of Col. John R. Chambliss—made contact with 6,000 U.S. troopers, the members of Brig. Gen. Judson Kilpatrick's 3rd Division, Cavalry Corps. Eager to brush aside Kilpatrick's men, Stuart fed reinforcements into the fight, and for several hours, the two sides grappled with each other, even taking the combat into the city streets.

The Battle at Hanover was unexpected and confusing. At one point, Stuart narrowly avoided capture when a squadron of Union cavalry overran his headquarters. Stuart and his staff rode to safety by making a daring leap over a fifteen-foot ditch. When Stuart became worried that he might lose his 125 captured wagons—the only trophies from his errant ride—he ordered a withdrawal. The battle resulted in 330 casualties. Although it paled in comparison to what would occur at Gettysburg, the Battle of Hanover was no minor affair. A New York chaplain recollected, "The dead and wounded of both parties, with many horses, lay scattered here and there along the streets, so covered with blood and dust as to render identification in many cases difficult." Stuart's men pulled back to the east, reaching a small borough called Dover, stealing horses from local farmers as they went. Still flummoxed as to the location of Ewell's infantry, Stuart planned to ride to Carlisle the next day, which, of course, would be in error, as Ewell's men had already planned to leave Carlisle that morning.

Back at Gettysburg, Buford made use of his cavalry's report of the encounter with Pettigrew's infantry. Through interrogations of Gettysburg civilians and information received from his scouts, Buford constructed a picture of the Confederate army. He correctly placed A. P. Hill's corps at Cashtown Pass (with Longstreet's corps behind it) and Ewell's corps coming down from Carlisle. Via couriers, Buford sent detailed reports to the Army of the Potomac's cavalry commander, Maj. Gen. Alfred Pleasonton, and also to Reynolds, whose 1st Corps—nearly 12,000 officers and men—was only seven miles to the southwest. Buford had completed his mission to locate the enemy, and as of the evening of June 30, he appeared to have much of Lee's position mapped out. He deduced that the bulk of Lee's army was heading in the direction of Gettysburg, but what should be done about it?

At Marsh Creek, Reynolds read Buford's reports with interest. Having already intended to move to Gettysburg under Meade's orders, Reynolds now declared that Buford needed support. He sent instructions to Brig. Gen. James Wadsworth, who commanded the 1st Division, 1st Corps, to get his men ready to move. Meade, too, read these same reports, and reached that same conclusion. Meade had been on the cusp of ordering Reynolds to take up his position at Pipe Creek, but now Meade decided to let the previous orders stand. Although the 3rd Corps could not be spared—as it had been ordered to hold Emmitsburg and watch the mountain passes—the 1st and 11th corps could both reach Gettysburg by midday. At 7 a.m., July 1, Reynolds summoned Doubleday to discuss the proposed movement. Reynolds did not expect any fighting to begin, but if the Army of Northern Virginia appeared, there must be no doubt about their mission. According to Doubleday, Reynolds declared his intent to "fight the enemy as soon as he could meet him."

THE FIRST DAY

THE CAVALRY SKIRMISH

The soldiers of Maj. Gen. Heth's division began marching at 5 a.m., July 1. Altogether, Heth brought about 7,830 men and twenty artillery pieces. Heth believed he had been given carte blanche to advance against the foe. He wrongly supposed that militia stood in his front, and he anticipated an easy encounter.

The Confederates trudged southeast along the Chambersburg Pike, churning up dust. At 7 a.m., the head of the column reached a rivulet called Marsh Creek. From his position atop Wisler's Ridge, Union Lieut. Marcellus E. Jones of the 8th Illinois Cavalry spotted the dust cloud. Borrowing a sergeant's carbine, Jones steadied it on a fence rail. Carefully, he fired at a mounted officer some 600 yards away, probably doing no damage. Years after the war, many Union veterans claimed to have fired the first shot of the battle, but Jones's assertion received the most attention. In 1886, veterans erected a marker on the spot, commemorating his "first shot" of the battle.

Within minutes, other Union videttes—about thirty of them along the sector occupied by the 8th Illinois—opened fire. Bullets whizzed at Heth's Confederates, and in response, the two brigades leading the column— Brig. Gen. James J. Archer's and Brig. Gen. Joseph R. Davis's—deployed skirmishers. Archer's and Davis's brigades advanced slowly, moving up the slope of Wisler's ridge. Meanwhile, Maj. William J. Pegram deployed a few cannon, which began hurling exploding shells against Buford's troopers in a frantic effort to scatter them.

Buford's videttes gave way, having no intent to fight for control of Wisler's Ridge. Many of his troopers had been on duty all night and their fatigued horses could not gallop. Mounting up before the Confederates closed the distance, Buford's men retired from Wisler's Ridge in good order. However, once the Confederates took the ridge, they found another line of cavalry awaiting them. Buford had put more than 200 skirmishers atop Herr's Ridge, one mile east. As Heth's infantry advanced again, Buford's skirmishers opened up, firing from behind stone walls and rail piles. Comparatively, Buford's men were well armed. Each trooper fired a single-shot breech-loading carbine. (Buford's division carried a mix of Sharps, Burnside, Smith, Gallagher, and Merrill breech-loaders.) Although not terribly accurate at long range, these carbines allowed dismounted cavalry to reload quickly and fire from behind cover. Armed with muzzle-loading weapons, the Confederates

The cavalry skirmish

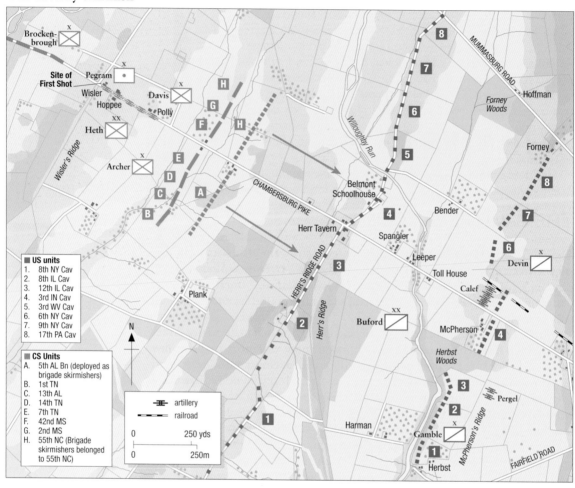

Legend — US units:
1. 8th NY Cav
2. 8th IL Cav
3. 12th IL Cav
4. 3rd IN Cav
5. 3rd WV Cav
6. 6th NY Cav
7. 9th NY Cav
8. 17th PA Cav

CS Units:
A. 5th AL Bn (deployed as brigade skirmishers)
B. 1st TN
C. 13th AL
D. 14th TN
E. 7th TN
F. 42nd MS
G. 2nd MS
H. 55th NC (Brigade skirmishers belonged to 55th NC)

artillery
railroad

0   250 yds
0   250m

had to reload from a standing position. Their weapons, however, possessed nearly triple the range of Buford's troops.

For the next hour, Heth's Confederates made slow progress, losing men as they trudged toward Herr's Ridge. Heth's exact losses are unknown. Probably fewer than fifty were hit and maybe none of them were even killed. Of course, the real contribution of Buford's cavalry came not from the casualties they inflicted but from the delay they imposed upon the Confederate advance. An Illinois officer assigned to Buford's division later wrote home to his local newspaper that, "We actually compelled them to halt and change their line of battle several times. The prisoners we took said they supposed our whole cavalry force was on their front and flanks." When Heth's division made first contact, his troops were three and a half miles from Gettysburg. After an hour of skirmishing, the Confederates had reduced that distance by only one mile. After Buford's line withdrew from Herr's Ridge, the survivors— those who still had ammunition and fresh horses—fell back to the third line atop McPherson's Ridge. In addition, these troopers received the support of Lieut. John H. Calef's horse artillery, six guns scattered across the ridge. (Specifically, four of Calef's guns were near the pike and two others farther south near the Fairfield Road.)

Once again, Heth's Confederates had to repeat their performance and drive out the pesky cavalrymen. Archer's and Davis's brigades halted atop Herr's Ridge. The men reformed their lines, reloaded their weapons, and cooled off. Although the day was not terribly hot, the exertion had fatigued more than a few of Archer's men. A nineteen-year-old Alabama soldier who survived the battle later recalled how he felt: "It was about nine o'clock in the morning and hot, hotter, hottest!" As Archer's men tried to catch their breath, Heth galloped onto the field and urged Archer to advance. Apparently, Archer questioned the wisdom of continuing the assault, worrying that his brigade (about 1,200 strong) was too small to deal with the federal force in his front. Evidently believing that he still confronted only token resistance, Heth ignored Archer's protest and told him to get going. Reluctantly, Archer cut short his men's respite.

Buford monitored the situation from the cupola of the Lutheran Theological Seminary. At about 9.30 a.m., Reynolds and his staff reached the Seminary to confer with Buford. According to the recollection of Buford's signal officer, Lieut. Aaron Jerome, when Reynolds reached the foot of the building, he spied Buford inside the cupola and called out to him: "What's the matter, John?" Sardonically, Buford replied, "The devil's to pay." Buford descended the steps and Reynolds gave him the news: he intended to stop the Confederate advance here at Gettysburg. Reynolds said, "I hope you can hold out until my corps comes up."

Buford looked out over the fields. McPherson's Ridge had not yet fallen; there was yet time to bring up the infantry of Doubleday's 1st Corps and reinforce the embattled position. Buford replied, "I reckon I can."

Apparently, Reynolds determined what to do after Buford briefed him. Based on orders sent to him from Meade, Reynolds had three options: First, he could withdraw to Maryland and cover Taneytown and Emmitsburg, the most cautious option. Second, he could screen the enemy with Buford and occupy the high ground south of Gettysburg, awaiting the arrival of reinforcements. Or, third, he could trade men for time by engaging the enemy beyond the town and screening the best terrain and the road network that would bring the rest of the army to his support. This was the riskiest option, but perhaps also the best.

Hastily, Reynolds fired off a message to Meade, sending a staff officer on a fourteen-mile ride to deliver it. Reynolds informed Meade of his intent to hold back the Confederate advance north and west of Gettysburg, vowing to fight "inch by inch." If driven into Gettysburg, Reynolds promised to barricade the streets and fight behind them. Reynolds also sent a mounted courier to find the 11th Corps commander, Maj. Gen. Oliver O. Howard, and order him to make his way to Gettysburg with all possible speed. If Buford's estimate was correct, Ewell's corps would be approaching via the Carlisle Road. The 11th Corps would be sorely needed to arrest its advance. Finally, Reynolds backtracked to the head of his infantry column—Wadsworth's division—and led it into the fray. Reynolds wished to deploy it personally.

At about this time, some of Buford's troopers had made contact with Ewell's corps north of town. Three of Buford's regiments—the 6th New York, the 17th Pennsylvania, and the 9th New York—stretched their vidette

Maj. Gen. Henry Heth commanded the C.S. infantry division that approached Gettysburg on the morning of July 1. Advancing down the Chambersburg Pike, Heth's infantry pushed back Buford's cavalry, but by midmorning, Reynolds's infantry had stopped them cold. Later in the day, a piece of shrapnel grazed Heth's head, forcing him to relinquish command. (Library of Congress)

The borough of Gettysburg numbered approximately 2,400 residents. This image of Gettysburg was taken on July 7, 1863, looking north from the roof of the Evergreen Cemetery, which sits atop the crest of Cemetery Hill. The Baltimore Pike is in the foreground. A bivouac belonging to an Emergency Militia Regiment can be seen at the right of the image. That regiment arrived on July 6 after the fighting had ended. The fields of the first day's battle were just beyond the town to the north and west, approximately 1.7 miles from where this photograph was taken. (Library of Congress)

screen in a wide arc between the Mummasburg Road and the York Road, over three miles from the center of town. Around 10 a.m., the first of Ewell's soldiers appeared atop a large acclivity called Keckler's Hill. These troops belonged to the division commanded by Maj. Gen. Robert E. Rodes. That morning, it had started from Heidlersburg, marching west along a road that connected it with Middletown (presently Biglerville). At Middletown, after being advised by Hill, Ewell finally realized how he must execute Lee's orders to proceed to "Cashtown or Gettysburg." The noise of Heth's encounter with Buford's cavalry made it evident that he must go to Gettysburg. Accordingly, Ewell ordered Rodes to turn his division south.

At Keckler's Hill, Rodes's scouts encountered Buford's vidette screen. (One of Buford's brigade commanders, Col. Thomas C. Devin, was in charge of this contingent.) Dismounted, the Union cavalrymen opened fire and Rodes promptly deployed countermeasures. Each brigade in Rodes's division possessed a "sharpshooter battalion," a 100-man unit commanded by a major. Three of Rodes's sharpshooter battalions deployed in skirmish formation and went to work, driving back the Union cavalry.

By 11 a.m., Col. Devin's advanced line could no longer stay where it was. Confederate numbers were so large that the Union cavalry had to retire to the edge of Gettysburg or risk capture. At the Harrisburg Road, two companies belonging to the 9th New York Cavalry barely galloped to safety when the bulk of Maj. Gen. Jubal Early's division appeared on their flank. At one point, a teenaged servant attached to that squadron—known only as Jim—had to race for safety. Jim had been doing laundry when his squadron made contact, and during his harrowing ride, the laundry flew out of his horse's nosebag. Remembered a veteran, "The enemy's bullets began to sing about him, he lay flat to his horse, the nosebag was flying and shirts, collars, drawers and stockings were scattered along the road and, no doubt these garments afterward did service for the Southern Confederacy."

All along the line, either north or west of Gettysburg, Buford's men began withdrawing. The skirmishers fell back to the "horse-holders," mounted up, and pulled back to safer environs. Col. William Gamble's brigade, which had borne the brunt of the morning fight, awaited the arrival of Wadsworth's infantry and then withdrew to the south side of the Fairfield Road. They hunkered down inside a woodlot owned by a farmer named McMillan. Meanwhile, Devin's brigade awaited the arrival of the 11th Corps. Once it reached the field, Devin pulled his men out of range, taking a position south of the York Road, near Rock Creek.

Buford's cavalry fought for three hours that morning, sustaining about sixty men killed, wounded, or captured. Probably, the Confederates who opposed them sustained fewer losses, but nonetheless, the Union cavalry offered an intangible contribution to the story of Gettysburg's first day. In resisting the Confederate advance for as long as they did, Buford's cavalrymen fatigued Heth's infantry and bought precious time for the Union infantry to take possession of the approaches into Gettysburg. If Robert E. Lee wished to stick to his plan and have his army coalesce at Gettysburg, he would now have to fight a prolonged engagement to do it. Had Lee accompanied Heth's advance, he might have called off further action, uniting his army at Cashtown. However, Lee was not present when Heth decided to press the attack. Unaware that Reynolds's infantry was in the process of replacing Buford's men, Heth drove Archer's and Davis's brigades forward, ultimately toward disaster.

THE MORNING ENGAGEMENT

The first Union infantry, Brig. Gen. James S. Wadsworth's 1st Division, 1st Corps, arrived on the battlefield supported by one battery of artillery, about 3,540 officers and men altogether. A wealthy gubernatorial candidate with unimpeachable courage, Wadsworth was ready for the fray. Having been advised by Reynolds, he ordered three of his regiments (the 56th Pennsylvania, 76th New York, and 147th New York) to cross over the unfinished railroad bed and enter a wheat field owned by James J. Wills. Meanwhile, Wadsworth directed his other regiments (seven of them) to form a line of battle along McPherson's Ridge on the south side of the railroad.

At 10.15 a.m., Heth's infantry began ascending the slope of McPherson's Ridge. Unwisely, the two brigades diverged from the pike—and from each other—as they attempted to outflank the position where Calef's guns had stood. Brig. Gen. Davis's rebel brigade made first contact with the Union infantry, opening fire on the 76th New York even before that regiment had formed into line of battle. Hunkering down in the wheat, the bluecoats allowed several volleys to whiz overhead. Soon, Davis's men closed to within 150 yards. "Is that the enemy?" wondered Col. J. William Hofmann, commander of the 56th Pennsylvania. Hofmann's brigade commander, Brig. Gen. Lysander Cutler, replied, "Yes." Quickly, Hofmann turned to his regiment and yelled, "Ready! Right-oblique, aim!" In the brief second right before Hofmann screamed "Fire!", Cutler wondered aloud if the enemy was even in range. The Pennsylvanians loosed a ragged volley. Cutler remembered, "I received my reply in a shower of rebel bullets by which many of the colonel's men were killed and wounded; my own horse and two of my

At approximately 10.45 a.m., July 1, as he was directing infantry at the east side of the Herbst Woodlot, a rifle ball struck Maj. Gen. John Reynolds in the back of his head. The projectile killed him instantly. One of Reynolds's orderlies, Sgt. Charles Veil, recollected, "He never spoke a word or moved a muscle after he was struck. I have seen many men killed in action, but never saw a ball do its work so instantly as did the ball that struck General Reynolds." Despite the confusion caused by Reynolds's death, his 1st Corps troops managed to repulse Hill's Confederates. (Library of Congress)

staff were wounded at the same time." More to the point, recalled Cutler, "the battle of Gettysburg was opened."

South of the railroad, Wadsworth's other regiments came in on the run, deploying *en échelon*. As each regiment came into line of battle, it charged west into the Herbst Woodlot. Although he was supposed to act as wing commander and supervise the action from the rear, Maj. Gen. Reynolds and his staff galloped close behind the 2nd Wisconsin, encouraging the men to give the rebels hell. One of the first incoming Confederate balls entered his skull behind his left ear, dropping him from his saddle. Reynolds's staff rushed to his side, hoping to revive him, but they discovered nothing could be done. The ball had killed him instantly. Several of his staff constructed a stretcher out of discarded blankets and carried their commander's body to the nearby Lutheran Seminary. Meanwhile, other staff officers fanned out to inform the other division commanders that Reynolds was dead. Frantically, they hurried to find Doubleday and tell him that he was in command of all Union troops on the field.

As Reynolds's staff officers galloped hither and yon, the Union counterattack continued on its own momentum. Two of Cutler's regiments—the 95th New York and 14th Brooklyn—held the McPherson farmyard to protect Capt. James Hall's battery, while four regiments belonging to Brig. Gen. Solomon Meredith's brigade—the 2nd and 7th Wisconsin, the 19th Indiana, and the 24th Michigan—moved west, firing at the Confederates, who were now readily visible through the smoke and underbrush. Eagerly, Meredith's men forged ahead, despite protests from the 1st Corps staff. When Capt. Craig Wadsworth (son of the general) rode up behind the 7th Wisconsin and shouted for it to halt, one of its officers mocked him, "It is now too late to halt!"

Initially, Archer's Confederates took advantage of their position inside the woods and along the banks of a stream called Willoughby Run, firing at Meredith's men as they crossed the open fields between the Seminary and McPherson's Ridge. The opening volleys of the 7th and 14th Tennessee culled as much as thirty percent of the 2nd Wisconsin's contingent. However, Archer's men soon realized they had bitten more than they could chew. "The

This photograph, which was taken in 1885, depicts Willoughby Run, the meandering stream where Brig. Gen. James Archer's brigade was routed by Brig. Gen. Solomon Meredith's "Iron Brigade." This perspective looks southwest from the Herbst Woodlot to the Emmanuel Harman farm fields. Because of postwar damming, the creek appears much wider than it did in 1863. The monument in the foreground belongs to the 19th Indiana, which lost about 20 men during the morning encounter. During the afternoon phase of the fighting, it lost another 190. (Gettysburg National Military Park)

firing was severe," remembered a Tennessee captain, "and the smoke of battle hovered near the ground, shutting out from view the movements of the Federal forces." Despite their initial losses, Meredith's men closed to within fifteen paces, delivering several well-aimed volleys. Archer's men began dropping, and those who were unhurt fell back steadily.

For several minutes, Archer's men looked to the rear, expecting reinforcements to arrive and relieve them from their predicament. When they backpedaled their way into Willoughby Run, their line broke. Dozens ran for their lives; those who stayed fell captive. Sensing an easy victory, Meredith's Midwesterners descended upon them like an avalanche. Lieut. Col. John Callis of the 7th Wisconsin remembered encountering a Confederate officer who rushed at him with a sword, blade first, saying, "I surrender." Using his own weapon, Callis knocked the sword out of his opponent's hand, replying, "That is no way to surrender!" Enraged, Callis took a second swing at the rebel but missed, saying, "If you surrender, order your men to cease firing, pick up your sabre and order your men to go to the rear as prisoners." The Confederate officer did as instructed, and Callis soon found himself herding more prisoners to the rear than he had soldiers under his command.

During the morning infantry fight, soldiers from the 2nd Wisconsin captured Brig. Gen. James J. Archer, a Maryland-born veteran of the Mexican-American War. For the next year, the U.S. Army held Archer in confinement at Fort Delaware and at Johnson's Island. In August 1864, Archer was paroled and exchanged, but he died two months later due to health issues incurred while a prisoner of war. (Library of Congress)

Even today, more than 150 years later, Confederate casualties in Archer's brigade are difficult to deduce. Archer's brigade fought on July 3, taking heavy losses during Pickett's Charge. Thus, the July 1 casualties cannot be differentiated from the July 3 casualties. During the whole battle, Archer's brigade lost 684 officers and men. Probably, as many as 300 fell during the fight with Meredith's brigade and perhaps as many as 100 of Archer's men (including Archer himself) were taken prisoner. Incidentally, Archer did not delight in his captivity. He held the distinction of being the first general from the Army of Northern Virginia to be taken in battle. When seized, a Wisconsin soldier tackled him roughly. Next, a Union officer forced Archer to relinquish his sword. Then, when he was trotted in front of Doubleday like a trophy, Archer exploded with profanity. Undoubtedly, many of Archer's veterans felt as he did, bitter at being forced to confront a brigade of federal infantry without support from the rest of the army. In 1925, one Alabama veteran, W. H. Moon, shared his opinion about the opening engagement. Moon had been captured on July 1 and spent fifteen months as a prisoner at Fort Delaware. At the conclusion of his account, Moon pointedly declared, "Archer's and Davis's brigades *alone* fought the battle on the morning of July 1, 1863."

North of the railroad bed, the situation went slightly better for the other Confederate brigade involved in the morning engagement, Brig. Gen. Joseph Davis's—at least initially. Cutler's three regiments suffered heavy losses as Davis's men advanced. Through Cutler, Wadsworth ordered these three regiments to execute a fighting withdrawal, but one regiment did not get out in time. The 147th New York's colonel was wounded just as the order was transmitted. The next officer in command, Maj. George Harney, failed to hear the directive, and soon, all three of Davis's regiments converged on the isolated New York regiment. As casualties mounted, Maj. Harney realized, on his own, what he should have done. He shouted, "In retreat—double-quick—march!" Unfortunately, most of his regiment fled in the wrong direction. The

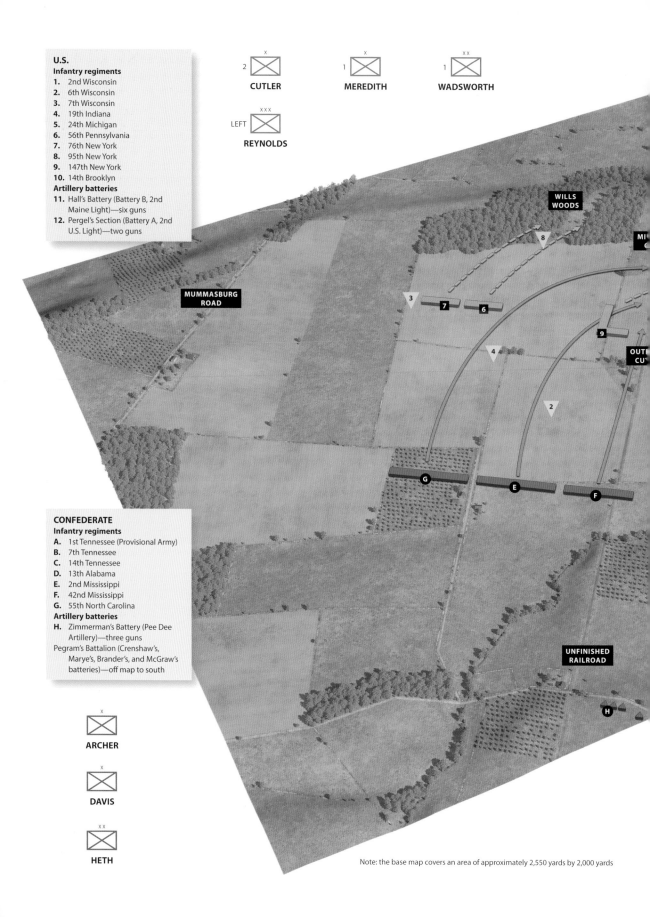

U.S.
Infantry regiments
1. 2nd Wisconsin
2. 6th Wisconsin
3. 7th Wisconsin
4. 19th Indiana
5. 24th Michigan
6. 56th Pennsylvania
7. 76th New York
8. 95th New York
9. 147th New York
10. 14th Brooklyn
Artillery batteries
11. Hall's Battery (Battery B, 2nd Maine Light)—six guns
12. Pergel's Section (Battery A, 2nd U.S. Light)—two guns

CONFEDERATE
Infantry regiments
A. 1st Tennessee (Provisional Army)
B. 7th Tennessee
C. 14th Tennessee
D. 13th Alabama
E. 2nd Mississippi
F. 42nd Mississippi
G. 55th North Carolina
Artillery batteries
H. Zimmerman's Battery (Pee Dee Artillery)—three guns
Pegram's Battalion (Crenshaw's, Marye's, Brander's, and McGraw's batteries)—off map to south

CUTLER

MEREDITH

WADSWORTH

LEFT REYNOLDS

ARCHER

DAVIS

HETH

WILLS WOODS

MUMMASBURG ROAD

UNFINISHED RAILROAD

Note: the base map covers an area of approximately 2,550 yards by 2,000 yards

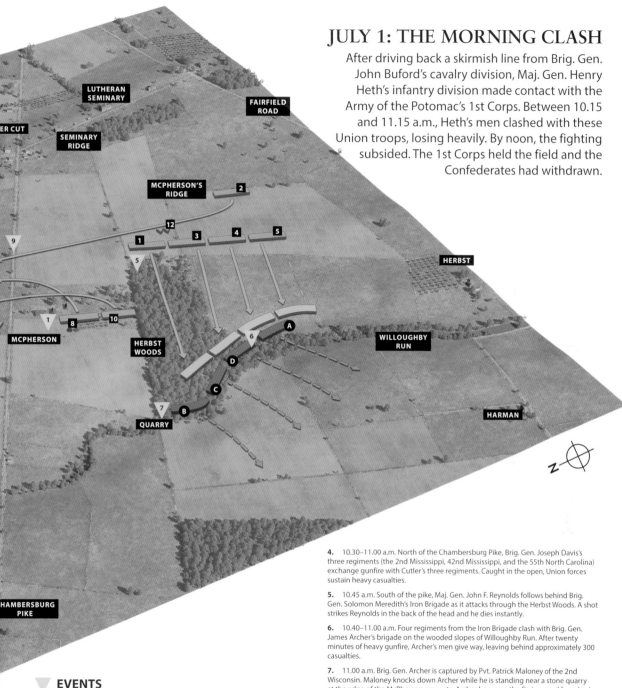

JULY 1: THE MORNING CLASH

After driving back a skirmish line from Brig. Gen. John Buford's cavalry division, Maj. Gen. Henry Heth's infantry division made contact with the Army of the Potomac's 1st Corps. Between 10.15 and 11.15 a.m., Heth's men clashed with these Union troops, losing heavily. By noon, the fighting subsided. The 1st Corps held the field and the Confederates had withdrawn.

LUTHERAN SEMINARY

FAIRFIELD ROAD

ER CUT

SEMINARY RIDGE

MCPHERSON'S RIDGE

HERBST

MCPHERSON

HERBST WOODS

WILLOUGHBY RUN

QUARRY

HARMAN

HAMBERSBURG PIKE

N

▼ EVENTS

(Times are approximate.)

1. 10.00 a.m. Union infantry from Brig. Gen. James Wadsworth's division reaches the Edward McPherson farmyard accompanied by Capt. James Hall's Battery B, 2nd Maine Light Artillery. The acting wing commander, Maj. Gen. John F. Reynolds, orders Wadsworth's men to counterattack.

2. 10.15 a.m. Heth's two brigades—under Brig. Gen. James Archer and Brig. Gen. Joseph Davis—advance from Herr's Ridge Road, heading east toward McPherson Ridge.

3. 10.30 a.m. One of Wadsworth's brigade commanders, Brig. Gen. Lysander Cutler, deploys the 56th Pennsylvania, 76th New York, and 147th New York on the John Forney property. When one of Heth's regiments (the 55th North Carolina) comes into range, the 56th Pennsylvania fires at it. This constitutes the first infantry volley of the battle.

4. 10.30–11.00 a.m. North of the Chambersburg Pike, Brig. Gen. Joseph Davis's three regiments (the 2nd Mississippi, 42nd Mississippi, and the 55th North Carolina) exchange gunfire with Cutler's three regiments. Caught in the open, Union forces sustain heavy casualties.

5. 10.45 a.m. South of the pike, Maj. Gen. John F. Reynolds follows behind Brig. Gen. Solomon Meredith's Iron Brigade as it attacks through the Herbst Woods. A shot strikes Reynolds in the back of the head and he dies instantly.

6. 10.40–11.00 a.m. Four regiments from the Iron Brigade clash with Brig. Gen. James Archer's brigade on the wooded slopes of Willoughby Run. After twenty minutes of heavy gunfire, Archer's men give way, leaving behind approximately 300 casualties.

7. 11.00 a.m. Brig. Gen. Archer is captured by Pvt. Patrick Maloney of the 2nd Wisconsin. Maloney knocks down Archer while he is standing near a stone quarry at the edge of the McPherson property. Archer becomes the first general from Lee's army to be captured in battle.

8. 10.50–11.05 a.m. Due to the severity of Davis's attack, Union forces north of the pike withdraw from the Forney fields. In semi-orderly fashion, the 56th Pennsylvania and 76th New York move out of range and into McPherson (or Wills) Woods. Caught on three sides, the 147th New York loses 296 out of 380 men before retreating south over the railroad. Capt. Hall's 2nd Maine Battery retires by section, temporarily abandoning one gun, which the gunners recover later in the afternoon.

9. 11.00–11.15 a.m. The 6th Wisconsin (with the "Iron Brigade Guard" attached) charges northward over the Chambersburg Pike, halting the advance of Davis's regiments. From their positions near the McPherson buildings, the 95th New York and 14th Brooklyn change front and join the 6th Wisconsin in its counterattack. Unable to withstand against this new threat, Davis's men retreat back to Herr's Ridge Road, losing fifty-five percent of their force. The three 1st Corps regiments capture approximately 150 of Davis's men at the railroad cut. Around 11.15 a.m. a short lull settles on the field.

Lieut. Col. Rufus Dawes commanded the 6th Wisconsin. Along with two other Union regimental commanders, he ordered a charge against Brig. Gen. Joseph Davis's brigade, which defended the middle railroad cut. During the charge, Dawes was abruptly thrown from his wounded horse, but he gained his footing, and led his regiment to the lip of the railroad cut, demanding the surrender of the Confederates trapped inside. Over 150 of them threw down their arms and became prisoners of war. (*Service with the Sixth Wisconsin Volunteers*, 1890)

56th Pennsylvania and 76th New York had withdrawn to the east, to the McPherson-owned woodlot. Harney's regiment could not follow suit, as one enemy regiment had got into its rear. Instead, the survivors of the 147th New York scrambled southward, descending into a massive railroad embankment. The Confederates pursued the New Yorkers and captured about ninety of them, those who descended into the deepest part of the cut. One New Yorker who scrambled into the cut (and then out of it) recalled, "While passing up the bank out of the cut, the bullets threw dirt in my face and over my hands, as I grasped hold of shrubs and sticks to assist me, they passed between my hands and body, around my head, between my legs, and all around me the bullets flew, and sounded like a lot of angry bees." By the end of it, the 147th New York had lost 296 out of 380 officers and men. The New York soldier who barely avoided the swarm of enemy bullets reflected, "How any of us escaped out of that trap alive, I cannot tell."

With Cutler's men in retreat, the 1st Corps officers south of the pike scrambled to check the Confederate advance. In a few minutes, staff officers belonging to Doubleday, Wadsworth, Meredith, and Cutler redirected three regiments—the 6th Wisconsin, the 14th Brooklyn, and the 95th New York—to the crisis point. They charged over the Chambersburg Pike to shore up Wadsworth's right flank. Davis's Confederates saw this new threat emerging. Although the railroad cut had practically doomed the 147th New York only minutes before, Davis's rebels now jumped into it and used it for cover. They clambered up the south slope and took shots from the grassy lip. After firing, the rebels ducked underground to reload. The 6th Wisconsin, in particular, took heavy losses as it crossed the road, which was bordered by a sturdy post-and-rail fence. Undaunted, the Yankees climbed it or bull-rushed it, snapping the rails loose.

Next, the three Union regiments crossed the deadly space between the road and the cut. They made their way to the edge, where hand-to-hand combat broke out along the lip. Too late, the Confederates realized they were in the same predicament the 147th New York had been in minutes earlier. Those in the shallow end ran out of it, heading northwest, back to Willoughby Run. Those in the deeper sections could not clamber out. Initially, they continued firing upward at their attackers. Union soldiers lined the edge of the cut, shouting: "Throw down your muskets! Down with your muskets!" Lieut. Col. Rufus Dawes, the commander of the 6th Wisconsin, shouted for the highest-ranking Confederate officer to identify himself. Maj. John A. Blair of the 2nd Mississippi stepped forward. Gesturing to his men, Dawes said, "I command this regiment. Surrender, or I will fire!" Maj. Blair said nothing. Quietly, he scaled the escarpment and handed Dawes his sword. With that, the remaining Confederates dropped their weapons and filed out of the cut, now prisoners of war. Dawes later remembered, "The coolness, self-possession and discipline which held back our men from pouring in a general volley saved a hundred lives of the enemy, and as my mind goes back to the fearful excitement of the moment, I marvel at it."

As with Archer's brigade, Confederate casualties among Davis's brigade on July 1 are difficult to deduce, but the three Union regiments probably captured between 100 and 200 enemy soldiers, including the flag and color bearer of the 2nd Mississippi. In the end, Davis's brigade was completely wrecked. The 2nd Mississippi started the day with 492 officers and men, but now only seventy men were available for duty. The other two regiments emerged better off, but together, they suffered about 960 losses, fifty-five percent of their July 1 roster. None of Davis's regiments were completely knocked out of action, however. Probably, as many as 754 men were still available to fight. Nevertheless, at that moment, those who were not taken prisoner or killed were sent fleeing to the rear. As the survivors of Davis's brigade and Archer's brigade (now under Col. Birkett D. Fry) withdrew out of range, a brief lull quieted the battlefield. The time was approximately 11.15 a.m.

During the respite, Maj. Gen. Doubleday assumed command of all Union troops on the field and contemplated his next move. Probably, he did not feel comfortable in exercising tactical command, since he immediately sent messengers to find Howard, the commander of the 11th Corps. As the senior officer, Howard had the responsibility of taking charge. But what to do in the meantime, Doubleday wondered, stay in position or withdraw through Gettysburg? Ever cognizant of how the battle would be interpreted by the northern press, Doubleday considered it wisest to remain in place. "To fall back without orders from the commanding general might have inflicted lasting disgrace upon the corps," he wrote, and as Reynolds had chosen to resist the Confederate attempt to enter Gettysburg, "I naturally supposed it was the intention to defend the place."

As he anxiously awaited news from Howard, the rest of the 1st Corps began to arrive. At 11.30 a.m., Brig. Gen. Thomas A. Rowley's 3rd Division arrived, and Brig. Gen. John C. Robinson's 2nd Division followed soon after. Doubleday directed Rowley to reinforce Wadsworth's division atop McPherson's Ridge while Robinson's division received orders to act as a reserve force along Seminary Ridge. While there, they began reinforcing their position by building a barricade made of rails and furniture. In addition, the remainder of Col. Charles Wainwright's artillery brigade rolled onto the field—another twenty-two cannon—and it spread along the line. Minus the casualties suffered in the morning engagement, Doubleday now had approximately 9,840 soldiers at his disposal.

As Doubleday realigned his troops, so too did his adversary, Henry Heth. Although Davis's brigade was all but in shambles, Fry's brigade (formerly Archer's) rallied on the south side of the Chambersburg Pike. Additionally, Heth's other brigades, Brig. Gen. Johnston Pettigrew's and Col. John Brockenbrough's, came within range, giving Heth another 3,500 troops. Those two brigades took up the forward line, deployed their skirmishers, and began taking long-range shots at the 1st Corps artillery. Behind them, atop Herr's Ridge, Hill deployed two battalions of artillery—thirty-three guns—under Maj. Pegram and Maj. David McIntosh. These cannon gained fire superiority over the nearby 1st Corps artillery. Pegram's guns fired over 3,800 rounds during the course of the battle, and probably the bulk of them were expended here.

Maj. Gen. Abner Doubleday took command of the 1st Corps after Reynolds fell dead. Equal to the emergency, Doubleday cobbled together a strong defense to cover the western approaches to Gettysburg. Although Doubleday led the 1st Corps competently on July 1, Meade replaced him on July 2, sending Doubleday back down to divisional command. Doubleday is depicted here alongside his wife, Mary Hewitt Doubleday. (Library of Congress)

This panoramic photograph was taken on July 15, 1863, looking east toward the borough from the middle of the 1st Corps' position along Seminary Ridge. Late in the afternoon of July 1, thousands of 1st Corps soldiers would be in retreat, passing through the view of this photograph, heading toward Cemetery Hill. The Chambersburg Pike can be seen running into the distance from the right foreground. The unfinished railroad can be seen running into the distance from the left foreground. The brick house at middle distance was owned by Elias Sheads and housed a girls' school called Oak Ridge Seminary. During the battle, the school principal, Caroline Sheads, quartered 72 wounded soldiers inside the dwelling. (Library of Congress)

Heth rested his men for more than an hour, and in the meantime, he reported news of the battle to his corps commander, Hill, telling him that his troops had encountered federal infantry. The "reconnaissance" was over. Not much is known about this meeting between Heth and Hill, so much of what historians believe to have transpired is based on conjecture. Circumstantial evidence suggests that Hill was keen to continue the attack. As soon as the next unit in the line of march, Maj. Gen. William D. Pender's division (6,680 aggregate), reached the battlefield, he intended to send Heth's fresh brigades forward. Professionally, it made sense. Hill knew that Ewell's men were on the way, and if Ewell's corps began its own attack, Hill would have to provide support.

By mid-afternoon, Lee arrived on the scene, apparently summoned by the sound of the fighting. At 11 a.m., Lee had departed Cashtown Pass, and for several hours, he trotted with his staff, passing wounded men who were streaming to the rear. By 2.30 p.m., he encountered Heth and Hill, who were conferring on the west slope of Herr's Ridge. The two generals were discussing the possibility of sending in the rest of Heth's division, followed by Pender's, when Lee abruptly stopped them. Miffed that both generals had elected to bring on an engagement without consulting him, Lee told them to cease all forward movement. There would be no further engagement, he declared, until Longstreet's corps came up. Then, as if to punctuate the awkward moment, the battle roared to life again. This time, it was not Hill's corps, but Ewell's corps. Lee had not known anything about Ewell's morning encounter with Union cavalry north of town, but now, it became clear that Ewell was engaging Union infantry as well. There are no primary accounts that described Lee's mood, but he must have felt frustration. Ewell was continuing a battle that Lee was trying to halt. Quickly, Lee rode to Ewell's front, seeking more information.

In about fifteen minutes, Lee encountered a staff officer who had come from Ewell's headquarters. Although it is not clear what, exactly, this officer told him, Lee probably learned that Ewell had two divisions available and that one of them was already engaging Union troops on Oak Ridge. Without meeting Ewell, Lee returned to Herr's Ridge. Back behind Hill's line, Heth repeated his request to attack. At this juncture, Lee relented, telling him he would receive permission momentarily. Those who were present at this meeting—Lee's personal secretary, Walter Taylor, among them—believed the prospect of battle had now become irresistible. "Neither side sought or expected a general engagement," Taylor recollected, "and yet, brought thus unexpectedly in the presence of each other, found a conflict unavoidable." Taylor was incorrect on two points. The Union army *had expected* an engagement. Indeed, Buford and Reynolds picked the field. Also, the battle *could have ended* then and there. With a show of authority, Lee could have reigned in his subordinates and called off further action; instead, he allowed them to press home their attacks.

Undeniably, this was a snap decision. But its importance cannot be overstated. In that exact moment, Lee determined that Gettysburg would be the place where he would seek out his decisive engagement. For the better part of a year, he had been searching for a battle that would change the trajectory of the war. Rolling the proverbial dice, Lee resolved that Gettysburg would be that battle.

OAK RIDGE

Shortly after noon, the head of the 11th Corps arrived on the field, catching up with its commander, Maj. Gen. Oliver O. Howard, who had preceded it to Gettysburg. A half hour earlier, Howard went to the roof of the Fahnestock Building at the corner of Middle and Baltimore streets to observe the conclusion of the fighting between Wadsworth's and Heth's troops. While there, he learned that Reynolds had been killed. Quickly, he rode to Cemetery Hill at the south edge of town to observe the deployment of his corps. According to protocol, he took over as wing commander. Howard's senior division commander, Maj. Gen. Carl Schurz, assumed command of the 11th Corps. According to Howard's own recollection, his first exclamation was to "stay here until the army comes." On the previous evening, Reynolds and Howard had discussed the possibility of engaging in battle, so Howard knew that fighting in the fields beyond Gettysburg was an option. He may not have come up with the idea on his own, but like Buford, Reynolds, and Doubleday before him, as acting field commander, Howard decided that Gettysburg was worth holding.

Howard placed one division from the 11th Corps—Brig. Gen. Adolph von Steinwehr's 2nd Division—in reserve atop Cemetery Hill, and then rode through town to assist Schurz in the deployment of the other two divisions. Howard and Schurz missed an opportunity to confer when Schurz was called away to deal with trouble at the north end of town. Two units—the 45th New York and Battery I, 1st Ohio Light artillery—were already opening up on Confederates near Oak Hill and Schurz needed to monitor the situation. The 11th Corps did not complete its deployment until 2 p.m., at which time, Howard and Doubleday met in person to discuss the situation. Both generals agreed that their small force needed to resist the impending Confederate attack, but if forced to retreat, they agreed that their two corps should consider Cemetery Hill as a suitable rallying point.

Overall, Howard's line was strong, but it had several vulnerable positions. One of those was Oak Ridge, which occupied the gap

At midday, Maj. Gen. Oliver Otis Howard assumed command of all Union troops on the field. A no nonsense evangelical who had already lost an arm in battle in 1862, Howard wisely selected Cemetery Hill as a fallback location. When the Army of the Potomac's line came apart at 4 p.m., Howard's forethought proved invaluable. His panicked soldiers found it a suitable place to rally. (Library of Congress)

At 1.30 p.m., Maj. Gen. Robert E. Rodes's division arrived at Oak Hill, perfectly poised to strike at the apex of the Army of the Potomac's line. Although Rodes commanded the largest division in the Army of Northern Virginia, he deployed it poorly. The division's opening assaults failed, leaving over 1,100 men killed or wounded. (Missouri Historical Society)

between the right flank of the 1st Corps and the left flank of the 11th. Doubleday believed he could not ignore this gap. At 1.30 p.m., reports from Devin's cavalry reached him, informing him about the arrival of Ewell's corps. In response, Doubleday ordered Brig. Gen. John C. Robinson to send one of his brigades from its position at the Seminary to occupy the gap at Oak Ridge. For this assignment, Robinson selected Brig. Gen. Henry Baxter's brigade, 1,450 strong. Baxter's men made a short jaunt, and as they emerged from the north edge of Wills Woods, they saw a Confederate attack materializing on the north side of the Mummasburg Road. Doubleday's and Robinson's decision to redeploy Baxter protected the threatened position in the nick of time. Quickly, Baxter put his troops into line. His brigade assumed the shape of a hairpin, with half of his men facing the road and the other half facing the John Forney farm fields. The men deployed in comparative safety under the east slope of Oak Ridge, out of view of the enemy. Only when Baxter was certain a collision was eminent, he ordered his troops to move to the crest of the ridge to engage the enemy.

The newly arrived Confederate troops confronting Baxter belonged to Maj. Gen. Robert E. Rodes's infantry division and Lieut. Col. Thomas Carter's artillery battalion. These units had been on the road all morning accompanied by their commander, Lieut. Gen. Ewell. As stated previously, they had already skirmished with Col. Thomas Devin's Union cavalry, driving them off.

Then, less than three miles from the edge of town, most of the division marched down Herr's Ridge Road, which took it to the north side of Oak Hill, the round northern protuberance of Oak Ridge. At some point, Rodes angled his men directly south, and they emerged from the scant tree cover to see the Forney fields before them. Rodes had made the decision to move to the ridge, evidently hoping to use it as a jumping-off point from which he could attack the Union 1st Corps, hitting it in its right flank.

Although Ewell was aware of Lee's directive not to bring upon a general engagement, he willfully ordered Rodes to attack the 1st Corps as soon as it came into view. Although the Yankees were not attacking, Ewell believed it was "too late to avoid an engagement without abandoning the position already taken up." Clearly, Ewell believed that to avoid an engagement was an error that Lee, who was not present, did not understand. Of his own volition, so Ewell later wrote, he "determined to push the attack vigorously." Without wasting any time, Carter's gunners unlimbered and opened fire upon the 1st Corps troops visible near the McPherson farm. From the perspective of Ewell, who accompanied Rodes to the north end of Oak Ridge, the position looked ideal. Not only were Carter's gunners providing exceptional support from the tree line, but Rodes's infantry could charge southward and sweep the 1st Corps troops from their positions near the railroad cut and the Chambersburg Pike. Neither Rodes nor Ewell, it seemed, realized the proximity of Baxter's troops, who were hidden nearby under the cover of the ridge on their left-front. Ewell told Rodes he had permission to engage.

Rodes's plan for a coordinated attack fell apart quickly. First, he had to dispatch one brigade toward the fields north of Gettysburg to deal with the arrival of the 11th Corps, a necessary precaution. Next, one of his other brigades disengaged prematurely. At the outset of his attack, Rodes directed

Col. Edward A. O'Neal to send three of his Alabama regiments—about 1,018 men—south across the fields of the Moses McClean farm and strike the Union line. For unclear reasons, Col. O'Neal did not accompany the attack, and according to Rodes, his men "went into action in some confusion." O'Neal's Alabamians stumbled awkwardly through the McClean wheat field, giving time for Baxter's men to take aim. After a few volleys, O'Neal called off the assault, apparently sending orders from his position in the rear. O'Neal later argued that he was forced to abort the attack because his men stood no chance against superior numbers of federal troops. After the battle, his superiors held him responsible for the brigade's poor performance. Rodes accused O'Neal of skulking in the rear. When Robert E. Lee learned of this, he retracted O'Neal's pending promotion to brigadier general. Whoever was at fault, O'Neal's casualties were staggering. Although figures are not precise, in its short engagement, O'Neal's brigade suffered somewhere between 200 and 300 casualties.

By not reporting his encounter to Rodes, O'Neal set the stage for a more tragic calamity. Another one of Rodes's brigades—Brig. Gen. Alfred Iverson's—trudged southeast from the crest of Oak Ridge and through the Forney farm fields. Iverson's men were unaware they were heading straight into the teeth of Baxter's troops. O'Neal's debacle had occurred on the east slope of Oak Ridge. Iverson's men, being on the western slope, saw nothing of the Alabamians' bungled attack. Covered by a stone wall and a thick grove of trees, Baxter's infantry remained hidden until Iverson's brigade closed to within point-blank range. When Iverson's North Carolinians were so close that the Union soldiers could even discern their facial expressions, the Union officers yelled, "Rise up men! And fire!" Baxter's soldiers stood up and volleyed, toppling the North Carolinians, who had no cover. Remembered a New York soldier, "Rarely has such a destructive volley been fired on any field of battle."

During the fighting, Robinson brought up his other brigade under Brig. Gen. Gabriel Paul and placed portions of it on either side of Baxter, bringing the total number of Union soldiers on Oak Ridge to nearly 3,000. The slaughter of Iverson's command continued on until after 2.30 p.m. when the Confederates began waving white handkerchiefs, pleading for mercy. In small clusters, Baxter's Unionists charged into the field, taking prisoners and capturing several regimental battle flags. At the end of the day, Iverson's brigade counted up 903 casualties out of 1,384 men brought into action. Although he was not entirely responsible for the appalling fate of his brigade, Iverson's reputation suffered. After the battle, Lee ordered him relieved of his command.

Rodes's attack had stalled. Two of his brigades—O'Neal's and Iverson's—had been repulsed with great loss, while two others had been drawn away to help other units. Only one brigade remained, Brig. Gen. Stephen D. Ramseur's, about 1,000 strong. With no other recourse, Rodes called Ramseur's North Carolinians from their reserve position and he ordered them to form on both sides of O'Neal's survivors, who were now reassembling atop the ridge. Over the next hour, Rodes and his staff prepared for this second attack. Bringing together O'Neal's men (including two regiments held back during the initial assault), Ramseur's fresh troops, and some rallied soldiers from Iverson's

At approximately 2.15 p.m., Brig. Gen. Alfred Iverson launched an assault with his North Carolina brigade. While passing through the Forney farm fields, Iverson failed to detect the presence of Brig. Gen. Henry Baxter's Union brigade along Oak Ridge. As a consequence, Iverson's brigade suffered 903 casualties out of 1,384 officers and men. Although Rodes had much to do with this disaster, in the aftermath, Iverson bore the blame. Shortly after the battle, Lee ordered him removed from the Army of Northern Virginia. Iverson is pictured here in a postwar photograph. (Library of Congress)

The fight at Oak Ridge, 2.00–4.30 p.m.

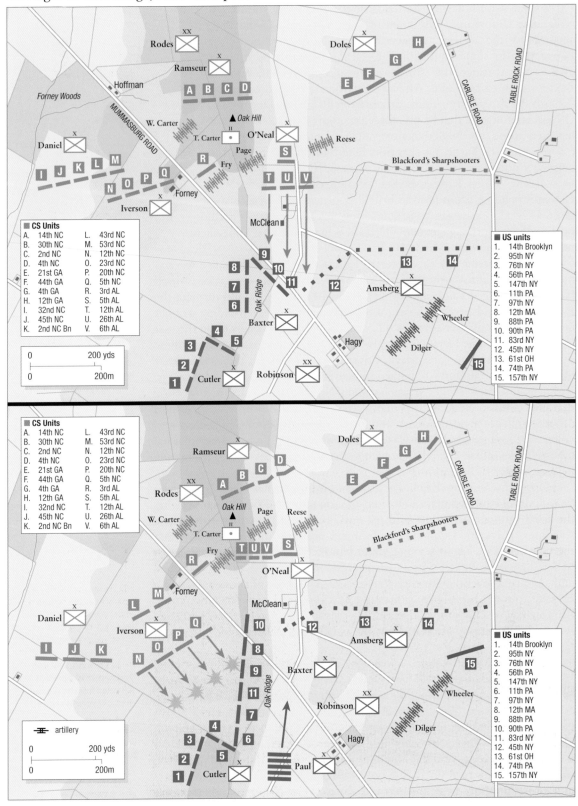

CS Units

A.	14th NC	L.	43rd NC
B.	30th NC	M.	53rd NC
C.	2nd NC	N.	12th NC
D.	4th NC	O.	23rd NC
E.	21st GA	P.	20th NC
F.	44th GA	Q.	5th NC
G.	4th GA	R.	3rd AL
H.	12th GA	S.	5th AL
I.	32nd NC	T.	12th AL
J.	45th NC	U.	26th AL
K.	2nd NC Bn	V.	6th AL

US units

1.	14th Brooklyn
2.	95th NY
3.	76th NY
4.	56th PA
5.	147th NY
6.	11th PA
7.	97th NY
8.	12th MA
9.	88th PA
10.	90th PA
11.	83rd NY
12.	45th NY
13.	61st OH
14.	74th PA
15.	157th NY

0   200 yds

0   200m

artillery

50

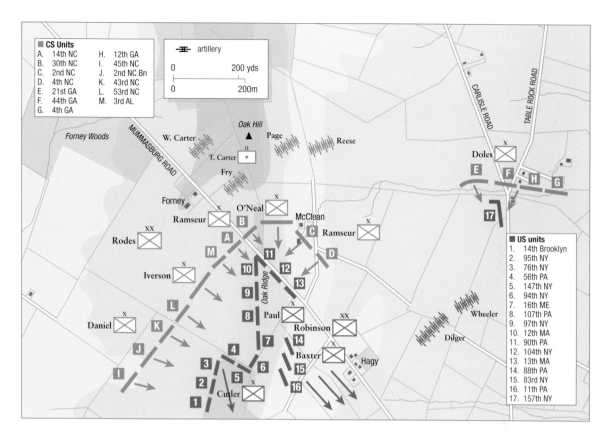

shattered brigade, Rodes beefed up the assaulting force to somewhere around 2,700 men. A little after 4 p.m., the division rolled forward again, facing a volcano of small-arms fire from Robinson's troops. Colonel Frank Parker of the 30th North Carolina, who ended the day with a gunshot wound through his face, wrote, "The fighting was of a desperate character."

In terms of manpower, Rodes's second attack almost doubled that of its foe. At this point, only Paul's brigade remained on Oak Ridge. During the lull between the two attacks, Robinson ordered Baxter's men to move

The 13th Massachusetts Infantry fought at Oak Ridge on July 1, losing 185 of its 284 officers and men. This image depicts a squad of enlisted men from Company C. They were photographed at Williamsport, Maryland, on November 21, 1861. One of the men in the image—Pvt. William F. Stoddard (third from left)—was separated from his regiment during its late-afternoon retreat. Initially, Stoddard's company commander listed him as "missing in action," but he surprised everyone by making his way through Gettysburg and rejoining his unit. (Library of Congress)

SURRENDER OF THE 16TH MAINE, 4.15–4.30 P.M. (PP. 52–53)

At 4.15 p.m., as the Union position north of town crumbled, Maj. Gen. Oliver Howard issued orders for the 1st and 11th Corps to fall back to Cemetery Hill. As Confederate infantry pressed their advantage, Brig. Gen. John C. Robinson's division (2nd Division, 1st Corps) experienced an untidy retreat from Oak Ridge (1), the wooded slope where the two Union corps joined together. Although one of Robinson's brigades made a clean break, the other one had to retreat under fire. Eventually, Robinson determined that one regiment from that brigade needed to stay behind and buy time for the rest to escape. Robinson selected the 16th Maine, instructing it to remain in place and to hold "as long as there was a man left." Before putting spurs to his horse, Robinson shouted, "Hold at any cost!" Turning to the officers near him, Col. Charles W. Tilden (2) said, "You know what that means." As the other regiments in its division filed off the field, heading south over the Chambersburg Pike, the 16th Maine advanced toward the enemy, occupying an exposed position designed to draw the enemy's attention.

Initially, the 16th Maine faced two Confederate brigades: Brig. Gen. Stephen Ramseur's North Carolinians and Col. Edward O'Neal's Alabamians. Two of Ramseur's regiments were on the left of the line, overlapping the Maine regiment's right flank. O'Neal's five regiments were in the middle and Ramseur's other two regiments were on the right. After twenty minutes or so, Col. Tilden ordered his men to commence a fighting withdrawal. His soldiers backed their way off Oak Ridge, firing at their opponents as they gave ground. When the 16th Maine reached the low ground at the eastern foot of the ridge, soldiers from Brig. Gen. Alfred Iverson's brigade (3)—about 400 of them—appeared atop the wooded slope. They, too, began firing into the Maine regiment.

The officers of the 16th Maine began looking over their shoulders, wondering if any other 1st Corps units would come to extract them. Lieut. Abner Small recollected, "But when they turned from the spectacle of the hosts advancing against them and looked anxiously to the rear, whence support and encouragement should be expected, they saw only the retiring columns of their companions in arms. It is remembered to the lasting glory of the officers and enlisted men of the Sixteenth that in this bitter moment not one of them wavered."

Sometime around 4.40 p.m., the 16th Maine backed its way to the edge of the inner railroad cut (4). As they reached that point, another Confederate regiment, the 43rd North Carolina (5), passed through the cut, nearly encircling the 16th Maine. Lieut. Small remembered that the "annihilation of the regiment as an organization seemed inevitable and immediate." The 16th Maine's two color bearers (6) tore the flags from their staffs, and with assistance from other soldiers, shredded them. They distributed the pieces among the men to prevent their capture. Meanwhile, a soldier from O'Neal's brigade approached Col. Tilden and ordered him to throw down his sword, "or I will blow your brains out." In defiance, Tilden jammed his sword into the dirt and broke the blade at the hilt.

On July 1, the 16th Maine had taken 275 officers and men into battle. During the engagement at Oak Ridge, eleven were killed, sixty-two were wounded, and 163 captured. About forty soldiers managed to escape. Col. Tilden remained in captivity for seven months. On February 9, 1864, he escaped Libby Prison in Richmond. After a harrowing flight through the Virginia backcountry, Tilden made it back to Union lines and rejoined his regiment.

back to their old position in the rear of Seminary Ridge to await an ammunition resupply that never came. Occupying the front lines, Paul's men now had the additional dilemma of facing an attack coming from two directions—north and west. To the Union soldiers, the new Confederate attack appeared unstoppable. In a few minutes, Union troops began falling by the dozen and several regiments gave way. Brig. Gen. Paul had his eyes sliced out by a musket ball, blinding him for life. After that, Paul's second-in-command fell wounded, and then the third-in-command was wounded and captured. Another officer in Paul's brigade, Lieut. Walter T. Chester of the 94th New York, recalled the confusion that reigned, "Then *sauve qui peut* [every man for himself] was the cry and out we went in inglorious confusion. To rally was impossible. On three sides of us a superior force hurled in a murderous volley ... How I escaped is miraculous. Once a man's neck saved me. His blood spouted all over me. Twice, horses intervened between me and wounds or death. But, thank God, I came through untouched."

Brig. Gen. John C. Robinson commanded the 2nd Division, 1st Corps. At Oak Ridge, his soldiers put up a dogged defense, but were eventually overwhelmed by Rodes's division around 4 p.m. (NARA)

Rodes's final push against Oak Hill occurred simultaneously with the Confederate attacks against the Union positions at Blocher's Knoll and Seminary Ridge (explained in other sections of this book). All along the Union line, Lee's infantry made a concerted push, and several positions began to crumble at once. Believing the game was up, Doubleday sent orders to all three of his division commanders to evacuate to Cemetery Hill. Robinson's division was the farthest away from the rallying point, so it was the first to commence its retreat. Union soldiers pulled off Oak Ridge at around 4.15 p.m. Lowest on ammunition, Baxter's brigade—which was now behind Seminary Ridge—withdrew first, followed by Paul's brigade, now under the command of Col. Richard Coulter. The retreat was not at all orderly. With Rodes's men advancing relentlessly, it became evident to Robinson that one regiment had to buy time for the others to escape. To that end, Robinson approached Col. Charles W. Tilden's 16th Maine, instructing it to remain in place and hold "as long as there was a man left." Initially, Col. Tilden objected; his regiment had fewer than 300 rifles. His men would be, at most, a mere speed bump. Tilden rejoined, "We may as well set up a corporal's guard to stop the rebel army." Robinson gave no advice. He repeated, "Hold at any cost!"

Alone, the 16th Maine stood against the bulk of Rodes's division. Looking over his shoulder, an officer from the regiment, Lieut. Abner Small, watched as the rest of his brigade filed off Oak Ridge bound for the streets of Gettysburg. Like others in his regiment, he knew what this movement signified. He wrote, "We were sacrificed to steady the retreat." For the next twenty minutes, the 16th Maine backed slowly out of the oak grove, the men firing as they backpedaled. The Maine soldiers reached the inner railroad cut, where the unfinished line passed through Seminary Ridge. Just as they reached the low ground east of the cut, a regiment of North Carolina troops poured through it, preventing the regiment's escape. In an instant, the bulk of the Maine regiment was surrounded. The two color sergeants asked permission to tear the flags into shreds and distribute them among the men to prevent their capture. Col. Tilden granted this request. Meanwhile, Tilden jammed his sword into the dirt, and with a herculean twist of his wrist, snapped it off at the hilt. Unable to fight their way out, 163 officers and men, including Col. Tilden, surrendered.

Col. Charles W. Tilden commanded the 16th Maine. After 4 p.m., Tilden received orders from Brig. Gen. Robinson to act as the division's rear guard. In order to buy time so the rest of the division could escape, Robinson ordered Tilden to stand firm as long as there were men available to fight. Around 4.30 p.m., Confederate troops surrounded Tilden's regiment. Although 60 soldiers from the 16th Maine managed to escape, Tilden and 162 others became prisoners of war. (Maine State Archives)

During the final attack against Oak Ridge, Rodes deployed elements from four of his brigades; however, Brig. Gen. Stephen D. Ramseur's brigade bore the brunt of the fighting. In driving Robinson's men from the field, Ramseur's brigade lost 26 percent of its attacking force. Ramseur survived Gettysburg unhurt, but he was mortally wounded at the Battle of Cedar Creek in October 1864. (Wikimedia Commons)

Brig. Gen. Junius Daniel commanded one of Rodes's brigades. Two of his regiments participated in the attack against Oak Ridge, assisting in the capture of the 16th Maine. The other three regiments became embroiled in the heavy fighting near the Edward McPherson farm. Daniel survived Gettysburg without injury, but he was killed during the Battle of Spotsylvania Court House in May 1864. (Wikimedia Commons)

Although it had taken three hours, Rodes's division had conquered Oak Ridge. Ramseur, who had his mare killed under him during the attack, wrote to his girlfriend (who was also his cousin), stating, quite accurately, "My glorious little Brigade has again covered itself with glory." Leading the attack on Oak Ridge, Ramseur's men had driven the enemy from the field, collecting about 700 prisoners from Robinson's division. However, Ramseur's brigade paid a heavy price, losing 275 officers and men, or 26.8 percent of its total. The other units that went into action also suffered heavily. Altogether, Rodes's division may have suffered as many as 1,900 losses on Oak Ridge. As the smoke settled, the worn-out Confederate infantry scattered across the fields to loot the dead or to rescue wounded comrades. The ghastly piles of corpses—wearing both blue and gray—appalled the survivors. A North Carolina officer later recollected that it was the only battle where he saw blood run in rivulets, "and that too on the hot dry ground." Another North Carolinian who lost his best friend wrote that, "toungs can not tell the horrors of that day."

McPHERSON'S RIDGE

As the bulk of Rodes's division became embroiled in the fight on Oak Ridge, only one brigade from that division managed to carry out the mission of striking the Union troops at the McPherson farmyard. This was the 2,161-man brigade commanded by Brig. Gen. Junius Daniel. At about 2.30 p.m., while being covered by artillery fire from Carter's battalion, Daniel's troops crossed over the Mummasburg Road. This was a bit later than when Iverson's brigade marched to its doom, but being farther to the west—the right flank of Rodes's line—Daniel's men did not come under fire from Robinson's division. Tromping through farm fields, toppling fence rails along the way, Daniel's men made slow progress. Then, when Daniel learned of Iverson's repulse, he detached two regiments to cover Iverson's retreat. These regiments engaged with Robinson's federals until the end of the Oak Ridge action.

With his other three regiments still holding tightly together, Daniel pushed southward to the railroad bed, taking losses from Union artillery as he did so. Then, the brigade began taking fire from the cut itself. A lone Union regiment, the 149th Pennsylvania, had taken shelter inside it. The bluecoats were hidden beneath the northern lip, resting on their arms. After his skirmishers fell back, the regimental commander, Lieut. Col. Walton Dwight, instructed his men to fire at the Confederates' knees, which thrust Daniel's brigade into some confusion. But not enough. The North Carolinians redressed their lines, surged on, and drove the 149th Pennsylvania from the cut. Many Pennsylvanians were killed trying to scramble up the south bank and others never got out except as prisoners, as one Pennsylvanian admitted, "for the foe was upon them before they could get clear of it." Embarrassingly, during the retreat, Lieut. Col. Dwight forgot to recall his regiment's color guard and thus the regimental banners were left behind. For the next hour, the five-man color guard remained trapped behind enemy lines. Later in the day, skirmishers from Davis's brigade found them, and after a desperate hand-to-hand struggle, every member of the guard was shot and both flags fell into enemy hands.

McPherson's Ridge, 2.30–4.00 p.m.

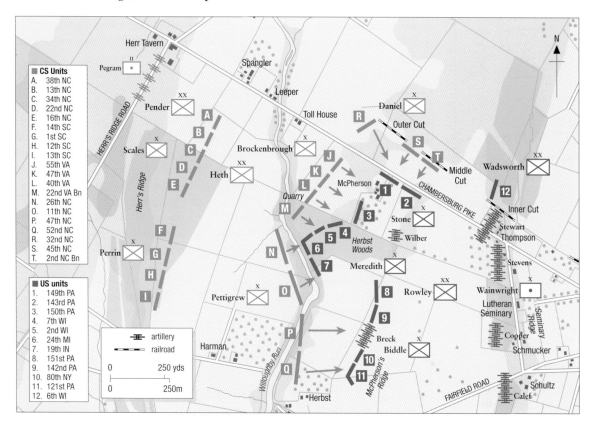

CS Units
A. 38th NC
B. 13th NC
C. 34th NC
D. 22nd NC
E. 16th NC
F. 14th SC
G. 1st SC
H. 12th SC
I. 13th SC
J. 55th VA
K. 47th VA
L. 40th VA
M. 22nd VA Bn
N. 26th NC
O. 11th NC
P. 47th NC
Q. 52nd NC
R. 32nd NC
S. 45th NC
T. 2nd NC Bn

US units
1. 149th PA
2. 143rd PA
3. 150th PA
4. 7th WI
5. 2nd WI
6. 24th MI
7. 19th IN
8. 151st PA
9. 142nd PA
10. 80th NY
11. 121st PA
12. 6th WI

artillery
railroad

0 — 250 yds
0 — 250m

With difficulty, Daniel's regiments separated into columns and his men crossed the shallow areas on either side of the cut. Once south of it, the brigade reformed its line, and moved toward the Chambersburg Pike. Union soldiers stationed at the McPherson farm watched all of this unfold. Col. Roy Stone commanded these troops, about 1,310 of them, including the 149th Pennsylvania which rejoined the brigade after retreating from its advanced position near the cut. As Daniel's men advanced, Stone's brigade (the 2nd Brigade, 3rd Division, 1st Corps) endured a murderous fire from Carter's artillery. With the exception of the McPherson house and barn, Stone's Pennsylvanians had no cover from the rounds coming from Oak Hill. Exploding shells were "falling in among us thick and fast," remembered a Pennsylvanian. When Daniel's men finally closed to within rifle range, many of Stone's Pennsylvanians were exceedingly happy about it, since it forced Carter's battalion to cease fire for fear of hitting their own men.

Stone did not exercise command for long. Just as the lines of battle made contact, he was wounded in the arm and hip, struck by several balls. His men dragged him into the McPherson barn for treatment and Col. Langhorne W. Wister assumed command in his stead. From behind the fence rails, Wister's three Pennsylvania regiments poured a deadly fire into Daniel's North Carolinians, stopping their advance. "The enemy approached within less than fifty yards," wrote a member of the 150th Pennsylvania after the battle, "when they were staggered by our fire and halted, exchanging shots with us for several minutes." Daniel thought he could flank Stone's position

Brig. Gen. James S. Wadsworth commanded the 1st Division, 1st Corps—the troops that held the center of the 1st Corps line. His soldiers engaged during the morning encounter and during afternoon fight at McPherson's Ridge. Portions of his division engaged in heavy combat on July 2 and 3 as well. Wadsworth brought 3,857 soldiers into the fight at Gettysburg, but lost 2,155 of them. A wealthy New York politician, Wadsworth survived Gettysburg, only to be killed at the Battle of the Wilderness in 1864. (NARA)

Edward McPherson, a former U.S. Congressman, owned a 66-acre farm on the south side of the Chambersburg Pike. On July 1, McPherson's house and barn became the center of the fighting. During the afternoon hours, Col. Roy Stone's Pennsylvania brigade held the farmyard, losing 850 officers and men in their attempt to resist the Confederate attack. This image depicts the McPherson farm on July 15. The scene looks north from the farm's south side. On July 1, the house, barn, and wagon shed would have been full of wounded men. (National Portrait Gallery, Smithsonian Institution; Frederick Hill Meserve Collection)

and sent one regiment, the 32nd North Carolina, west of the outer cut. Five companies from the 150th Pennsylvania (the regiment's right wing) met this regiment at the pike, stopping the advance cold. The 150th Pennsylvania then counterattacked across the meadow, driving the North Carolinians further still.

Daniel's men did not rout, however. They regrouped and launched a second assault, but Wister's Pennsylvanians repulsed this attack as well. Twice defeated, Brig. Gen. Daniel elected to change course. Now, he directed his three regiments to rejoin the 43rd and 53rd North Carolina, the two regiments he had detached to assist Iverson. Reunited, his brigade participated in the final push against Oak Ridge; however, the two fruitless attacks against Wister's Pennsylvanians had been costly. More than forty percent of his brigade had fallen casualty.

As soon as Daniel's men withdrew out of range, Carter's battalion opened up on Wister's Pennsylvanians yet again, and then, sometime after 3.15 p.m., Heth's division made its second attack of the day. Heth's two fresh brigades—Pettigrew's and Brockenbrough's—took the center of the advance, while Fry's brigade provided assistance on the right flank. Brockenbrough's brigade—971 aggregate—confronted Wister's men and also a portion of Meredith's brigade in the Herbst Woods. From Willoughby Run, it advanced up the slope of McPherson's Ridge but then came under fire from the 2nd and 7th Wisconsin and left wing of the 150th Pennsylvania. Capably, Wister redeployed the right wing of the 150th back to its old position, and with this volume of fire, Brockenbrough's brigade went to ground. Not long after this new gunfight started, a ball struck Wister in the face, disabling him. Unable to speak clearly, he turned over command to Col. Edmund Dana.

All along the Pennsylvanians' line, casualties piled up. Seventeen-year-old drummer Henry M. Kieffer recalled multiple heart-wrenching scenes around the McPherson farm. He wrote, "All over the field are strewn men, wounded or dead, and comrades pause a moment in the mad rush to catch the last words of the dying." Kieffer arrived in time to hear the final gasps of one of his friends, Corp. William E. Henning. Kieffer asked breathlessly, "Why Willie! Tell me where you are hurt!" Henning replied, "Here in my side, Harry. Tell mother—mother—" And with that, Henning expired. Dana's brigade (earlier Wister's, and before that, Stone's) suffered 853 casualties at Gettysburg, sixty-four percent of its total. Nearly all these

were cut down at the McPherson yard. Shortly before 4 p.m., when it became clear that the other 1st Corps brigades were retiring toward the Lutheran Seminary, Col. Dana ordered a withdrawal. Incredibly, Dana's men pulled back in good order, pausing to fire volleys to keep the Confederates at bay. At various points, a young color bearer with the 143rd Pennsylvania, Sgt. Benjamin H. Crippen, stopped to shake his fist at the oncoming Virginians, until an unlucky musket ball killed him. With stoic determination, another Pennsylvanian picked up the flag and bore it from Crippen's corpse. Lieut. Gen. Hill, who monitored the advance from behind Brockenbrough's men, witnessed Crippen's death. Turning to another officer, he casually remarked, "The Yankees have fought with a determination unusual to them."

As Heth's division made its second advance of the day, bloodshed occurred elsewhere along McPherson's Ridge, in what might rightly be called the bloodiest fighting of the entire battle. Two large regiments, the 11th and 26th North Carolina (both from Pettigrew's brigade), advanced into the Herbst Woodlot, following the path taken by Archer's brigade five hours earlier. Two Virginia regiments provided limited support. For the next forty minutes, the North Carolinians blazed away at four of Meredith's Midwestern regiments, which still occupied the same position they had taken during the morning engagement.

Known colloquially as the "Iron Brigade," Meredith's men pledged to hold the position at all hazards. However, numbers were not in their favor. These four regiments (the 19th Indiana, the 24th Michigan, and the 2nd and 7th Wisconsin) had started the day with 1,485 officers and men, but the morning encounter with Archer's brigade had subtracted 100 or more men from their ranks. Probably, they faced as many as 2,000 Confederates. Pvt. William Roby Moore of the 19th Indiana later claimed, "there was not a man in the ranks but realized the futility of endeavoring to turn back that horde." Moore's regiment lost only twenty men during the morning attack, but now, under intense fire from the 11th North Carolina, another 190 men were hit. Eleven soldiers were killed or wounded merely trying to keep the regiment's two flags aloft. Under withering fire, the 19th Indiana crumbled, followed by the 24th Michigan, which lost 363 of its 496 soldiers. Then, when Meredith ordered the surviving soldiers to withdraw to Seminary Ridge, casualties rose sharply in the two Wisconsin regiments. Capt. Hollon Richardson, of the brigade staff, who carried the extraction order to each of the regiments, later explained: "like dew before the morning, our men wilted away."

In two combat encounters, the Iron Brigade lost sixty-three percent of its number, leaving Herbst Woods full of dead and dying men. An Indiana officer, Capt. William Orr, wrote that the dead were "piled up on the ground, and the shrieks and groans of the wounded was too horrible for contemplation." Meredith himself was among the wounded, concussed by shrapnel fragments and injured when his horse fell on top of him. Unable to stay on the field, he relinquished command of the Iron Brigade to Col. William Robinson. Another Union regiment, the 151st Pennsylvania, covered the Iron Brigade's withdrawal southeast of the woods, paying a high price for it. (Company D of that regiment lost twelve killed and eleven wounded out of thirty-eight muskets, and other companies suffered similarly.)

Finally victorious, Heth's men inherited this bloodstained ground. A lieutenant in the 26th North Carolina wrote home that, "Neither language nor pen can describe the scene. The enemy was strewn in piles—some in

Corporal Franklin W. Lehman belonged to Company C, 149th Pennsylvania. During the battle, he carried one his regiment's two battle flags. While positioned north of the McPherson farm, the 149th Pennsylvania's color guard became embroiled in a fierce fight when two squads of Confederates attempted to capture the flags. Lehman was wounded in the legs and his flag was taken. He survived the battle and served out the remainder of his term of enlistment with the Veteran Reserve Corps. In this image, Lehman can be seen wearing his regiment's distinctive headgear, a forage cap adorned with a buck tail. (Library of Congress)

THE FIGHT AT THE EDWARD McPHERSON BARN, 3.30 P.M. (PP. 60–61)

At approximately 3.30 p.m., Confederate forces assailed the Union position at the Edward M. McPherson farm, a sixty-six acre plot along the Chambersburg Pike. Col. Roy Stone's brigade (the 2nd Brigade, 3rd Division, 1st Corps)—popularly known as the Pennsylvania Bucktails—defended this sector. Two regiments—the 143rd and 149th Pennsylvania—stood behind a rail fence line on the south side of the pike, facing north. Stone's third regiment—the 150th Pennsylvania—faced west, perpendicular to the pike. Shortly after the Confederates began their advance, Col. Stone suffered gunshot wounds to his arm and hip. As helpful soldiers dragged him to cover, Col. Langhorne Wister assumed command of the brigade.

During the battle, no civilians occupied the farm, which consisted of three structures: a barn (**1**), a one-story house, and a wagon shed (**2**). McPherson was a former U.S. Congressman, who had lost his seat in the Election of 1862. Three months prior to the battle, he took up residence in Washington D.C. to become deputy commissioner of the office of internal revenue. In 1863, a tenant farmer named John Slentz lived on the farm, but he fled shortly before the battle started. As the battle transpired, Union stretcher bearers began filling the structures with wounded men. By battle's end, dozens of sufferers—perhaps hundreds—had been abandoned on the property. Some of them remained on the farm for weeks until they could be safely moved.

On the afternoon of July 1, three regiments from Brig. Gen. Junius Daniel's brigade—the 32nd North Carolina, the 45th North Carolina, and the 2nd North Carolina Battalion—attacked Wister's Pennsylvanians. Daniel's men started from their position on the John Forney farm, moving forward at 2.30 p.m. The Pennsylvanians repulsed two assaults, forcing the North Carolinians to take cover inside a railroad embankment along the north side of the pike. But then, at 3.30 p.m., Maj. Gen. Henry Heth ordered his division to make a supporting assault from the west. Two of Heth's regiments—the 47th Virginia (**3**) and the 55th Virginia (**4**) of Col. John Brockenbrough's brigade—attacked the 150th Pennsylvania (**5**). With the arrival of Heth's division, the 32nd North Carolina (**6**) again surged across the pike, assaulting the 149th Pennsylvania (**7**) for a third time. Although casualties piled up and Col. Wister fell wounded by a gunshot to the face, the Pennsylvanians did not panic. At 4.00 p.m., their new commander, Col. Edmund Dana, conducted the entire brigade to Seminary Ridge in good order. With that, the fighting at the farm drew to a close.

The Bucktails had started the day with 1,317 officers and men. They lost about 850 killed, wounded, or captured. The Confederates also suffered heavily. At dawn, the 47th Virginia numbered 209 officers and men and it lost about forty soldiers on July 1. Meanwhile, the 55th Virginia took 268 officers and men into battle and it, too, lost about forty men. Finally, the 32nd North Carolina numbered 454 officers and men and it lost 181 of them.

At 3.15 p.m., four regiments from Virginia and North Carolina attacked Union 1st Corps troops stationed inside Herbst Woods. Two of those regiments, the 11th and 26th North Carolina, suffered heavy casualties, about 900 killed and wounded between them. This image depicts the regimental band of the 26th North Carolina. (Wikimedia Commons)

rows just as literally blue." Like so many successful Confederate attacks on July 1, the fight for Herbst Woods cost the Army of Northern Virginia a great deal. The four regiments that assaulted it—the 22nd Virginia Battalion, the 40th Virginia, and the 11th and 26th North Carolina—left behind approximately 1,000 dead and wounded in the same territory, one of every two rebels who fought.

This was not the last of it, either. Just south of the Herbst Woods, two more of Pettigrew's regiments—the 47th and 52nd North Carolina—made an assault against Col. Chapman Biddle's brigade from Rowley's 3rd Division, 1st Corps. Unlike the Iron Brigade, Biddle's 1,360 Pennsylvanians and New Yorkers had no cover. They held the crest of the barren southern end of McPherson's Ridge, anchoring the 1st Corps' flank with the Fairfield Road. The advance of the two North Carolina regiments had been slowed by Biddle's skirmishers, who were posted west of Willoughby Run. In fact, the skirmishers proved so annoying that the North Carolinians chose to burn the nearby Emmanuel Harman farm so it could not be used by the bluecoats in the event that Heth's attack failed. In looting the house and barn, the North Carolinians displaced the Harmans' teenaged daughter and her aunt, who were hiding in the cellar. After that, they set the farm ablaze. They also burned John Herbst's barn and would have burned his house as well except that several wounded Confederates had taken shelter there and could not be moved.

After pushing east across Willoughby Run, the two North Carolina regiments engaged Biddle's line of battle. Despite their disadvantageous position, the 47th and 52nd advanced with exceptional discipline. Biddle's men took aim from behind their meager coverings, high grass and piled fence rails; however, this gunfire did not deter the Confederates one iota. Hunkered behind a low fence along with the rest of his regiment, a soldier in the 121st Pennsylvania later explained, "Great gaps in their lines were closed as fast as [we] created [them], and still they came on. Still both of their lines overlapped ours by at least two regiments, and as they swung round our loss was very severe."

The Union brigade commander, Biddle, rode back and forth along the lines, encouraging his men, seemingly oblivious to danger as the bullets zipped around him. Eventually, one bullet wounded Biddle's horse. In a panic, it tossed him and he fell to the ground with an ugly thump. Struggling to his feet, he wandered to the rear,

Forty-one-year-old Col. Chapman Biddle commanded the 1st Brigade, 3rd Division, 1st Corps. He made himself conspicuous on July 1 by riding up and down the line, encouraging his men. A captain in his brigade remembered, "Throughout this tornado of fire he rode back and forth along the line of his brigade, and by his daring, by his apparent forgetfulness of his own danger, accomplished wonders with his four small regiments." A Confederate ball wounded him slightly on the head and his wounded horse threw him to the ground. Despite his head wound, Biddle continued to direct his brigade. He is pictured here in a postwar photograph. (*History of the 121st Regiment Pennsylvania Volunteers*, 1905)

This photograph depicts the officer corps of the 80th New York, a 1st Corps regiment that fought at the south end of the Union line. At the Battle of Gettysburg, it lost 170 of its 287 officers and men. After the battle, a newspaper in Ulster, New York (the regiment's hometown), remarked, "Peace to the memories, felicity to the spirits, of those who laid down their lives in repelling rebel invasion. Universal gratitude, lifelong honor, to those who, scarred or maimed, passed through the harvest of death." (Library of Congress)

seeking medical attention. The commander of the 121st Pennsylvania, Maj. Alexander W. Biddle (a cousin to Chapman), wrote: "[the Confederates] came on beautifully in perfect order until just as their heads showed over the grain on top of the hill—we poured in a volley receiving a severe fire in return—outnumbered by a double line we fought hard [and] gave them fire for fire but found them coming up on our left. The[y] were not more than 30 yds off firing on us briskly."

At the height of the engagement, Maj. Biddle also lost his horse, named "Transportation." Thrice wounded by musket balls, Transportation became uncontrollable. Biddle dismounted and tried to calm him, but at that moment, his cousin's horse, having thrown its rider, came careening toward him, frothing and frantic. Amazingly, Biddle caught the errant horse by the reins, but Transportation became alarmed, pulled free from Biddle's grip, and galloped to the rear. As his faithful mount disappeared into the smoke, Biddle's heart sank. He could see his men falling fast. Reluctantly, Maj. Biddle ordered the survivors to retire to the Lutheran Seminary, where a barricade of rails had been earlier piled up by the 2nd Division. Biddle later admitted that his men did not quit the field in good order. Outflanked,

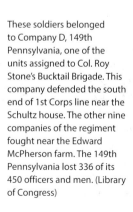

These soldiers belonged to Company D, 149th Pennsylvania, one of the units assigned to Col. Roy Stone's Bucktail Brigade. This company defended the south end of 1st Corps line near the Schultz house. The other nine companies of the regiment fought near the Edward McPherson farm. The 149th Pennsylvania lost 336 of its 450 officers and men. (Library of Congress)

they broke formation and ran pell-mell toward the Seminary. Naturally, this compelled the other three regiments in the brigade to fall back as well; although, they needed no further encouragement. The commander of the 151st Pennsylvania later wondered how his men could fight in such an "unequal contest." Like most 1st Corps units on July 1, Biddle's brigade sustained more than sixty percent losses before withdrawing.

On the Confederate side, losses were equally staggering. The attack against McPherson's Ridge had cost Heth's division approximately 2,000 officers and men. But, at 4 p.m., the ridge was, at last, in their hands. Although he was no longer alive to see it, Reynolds's scheme to trade men for time was costing the Confederates dearly.

THE ROUT OF 11TH CORPS

As the 1st Corps defended the approaches west of Gettysburg, another corps—the 11th—took up the task of protecting the two roads that entered Gettysburg from the north, the Carlisle Road and the Harrisburg (Heidlersburg) Road. By 1.45 p.m., the 1st and 3rd divisions of the 11th Corps commenced their deployment. Brig. Gen. Alexander Schimmelfennig's 3rd Division straddled the Carlisle Road with two artillery batteries supporting it. Meanwhile, Brig. Gen. Francis C. Barlow's 1st Division took up a position atop Blocher's Knoll—a small hillock at the edge of Rock Creek—with one battery to support him.

Arguably, the generals in the 11th Corps did not use the terrain north of town to their advantage. Ultimately, poor deployment of their troops led to a massive retreat later in the afternoon. No single decision made by the 11th Corps elicited as much controversy as Barlow's decision to take possession of the knoll, particularly since it was a third of a mile ahead of the nearest infantry. Several 1863 newspapers—and later, a legion of twentieth-century historians—singled out this movement as the greatest mistake made by the Army of the Potomac on July 1.

Even today, the source of the Union's error is difficult to discern. In part, Barlow appears to have moved there accidentally. Initially, his division took position on either side of the Harrisburg Road, near the county alms house. But his men were not deployed for long before they came under fire from a sharpshooter battalion belonging to Brig. Gen. George P. Doles's brigade, which was positioned inside the woods north of Blocher's Knoll. To deal with this threat, Barlow sent Col. Leopold von Gilsa's brigade to drive it off. After doing so, Barlow ordered the rest of his division to follow.

Immediately after the battle, Barlow explained that he had merely followed orders given to him, forming his division "as directed" by the corps commander, Maj. Gen. Schurz. However, Schurz later maintained that he never instructed Barlow to advance so far out, but instead, ordered him to extend the line of the 3rd Division, which sat at the edge of the town. Both Barlow and Schurz were capable officers, and after the battle, none of their colleagues ever censured them.

Apparently, some form of miscommunication occurred. Either Schurz garbled his instructions to Barlow or Barlow

Brig. Gen. Francis C. Barlow commanded the 1st Division, 11th Corps. In mid-afternoon, he advanced his division to Blocher's Knoll, a small hill that overlooked Rock Creek. At 3.45 p.m., Confederate forces under Ewell easily swept Barlow's troops off the knoll, and Barlow himself received a serious wound to the abdomen and was captured. Amazingly, Barlow recovered from his wound, returned to the army, and ended the war as a major general. After the battle, his decision to deploy atop the knoll elicited controversy. (Library of Congress)

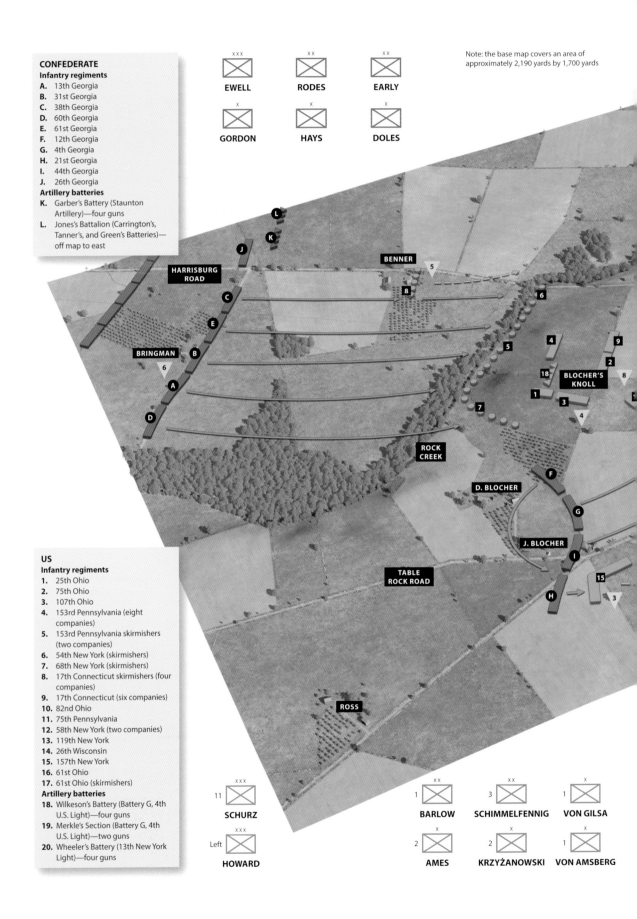

CONFEDERATE
Infantry regiments
A. 13th Georgia
B. 31st Georgia
C. 38th Georgia
D. 60th Georgia
E. 61st Georgia
F. 12th Georgia
G. 4th Georgia
H. 21st Georgia
I. 44th Georgia
J. 26th Georgia
Artillery batteries
K. Garber's Battery (Staunton Artillery)—four guns
L. Jones's Battalion (Carrington's, Tanner's, and Green's Batteries)—off map to east

Note: the base map covers an area of approximately 2,190 yards by 1,700 yards

EWELL
RODES
EARLY
GORDON
HAYS
DOLES

HARRISBURG ROAD
BENNER
BRINGMAN
BLOCHER'S KNOLL
ROCK CREEK
D. BLOCHER
J. BLOCHER
TABLE ROCK ROAD
ROSS

US
Infantry regiments
1. 25th Ohio
2. 75th Ohio
3. 107th Ohio
4. 153rd Pennsylvania (eight companies)
5. 153rd Pennsylvania skirmishers (two companies)
6. 54th New York (skirmishers)
7. 68th New York (skirmishers)
8. 17th Connecticut skirmishers (four companies)
9. 17th Connecticut (six companies)
10. 82nd Ohio
11. 75th Pennsylvania
12. 58th New York (two companies)
13. 119th New York
14. 26th Wisconsin
15. 157th New York
16. 61st Ohio
17. 61st Ohio (skirmishers)
Artillery batteries
18. Wilkeson's Battery (Battery G, 4th U.S. Light)—four guns
19. Merkle's Section (Battery G, 4th U.S. Light)—two guns
20. Wheeler's Battery (13th New York Light)—four guns

11 SCHURZ
Left HOWARD
1 BARLOW
3 SCHIMMELFENNIG
1 VON GILSA
2 AMES
2 KRZYŻANOWSKI
1 VON AMSBERG

JULY 1: BLOCHER'S KNOLL

During the midafternoon, two Confederate infantry brigades assaulted the position held by the Army of the Potomac's 11th Corps. The 1st Division, 11th Corps, had taken up a weak position atop Blocher's Knoll, a treeless hill located between the Carlisle and Harrisburg roads. When the 1st Division routed, the acting wing commander, Maj. Gen. Oliver Howard, could not scramble sufficient reinforcements to the threatened area in time. Reluctantly, Howard ordered his soldiers to retreat through town and rally atop Cemetery Hill, where 2nd Division, 11th Corps, sat in reserve. The success of the Confederate attack against the Union position at Blocher's Knoll turned the tide in Lee's favor.

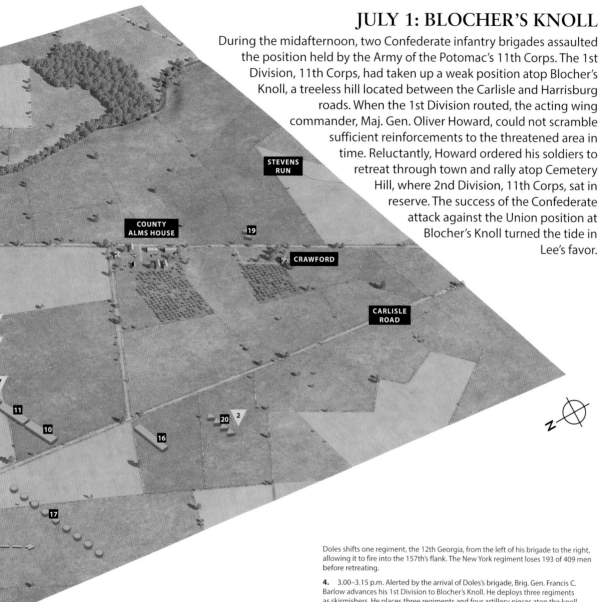

STEVENS RUN

COUNTY ALMS HOUSE

19

CRAWFORD

CARLISLE ROAD

9

7

11

10

20 2

16

17

▼ EVENTS

(Times are approximate.)

1. 1.45–2.00 p.m. Two divisions from the 11th Corps, the 1st and 3rd divisions, deploy along the northern edge of town. Initially, the 3rd Division holds the ground between the Carlisle Road and the Mummasburg Road. The 1st Division sits astride the Harrisburg Road. The 3rd Division deploys three regiments of skirmishers toward the David Hagy and Moses McClean farms.

2. 2.15–2.45 p.m. Maj. Gen. Robert Rodes's division arrives atop Oak Hill (off map), deploying Lieut. Col. Thomas Carter's artillery battalion along the hill's southeast slope. Carter's gunners duel with two 11th Corps batteries: Capt. Hubert Dilger's (Battery I, 1st Ohio Light) and Lieut. William Wheeler's (13th New York Light). The Confederate artillery suffers the worst of this exchange.

3. 2.45–3.00 p.m. At the Moses McClean farm (off map) the 45th New York captures dozens of Confederates belonging to Rodes's division. This causes the 45th's brigade commander, Col. George von Amsberg, to advance more infantry to its support. In consequence, the regiment on the right of von Amsberg's line, the 157th New York, runs into trouble. At the intersection of the Carlisle and Table Rock roads, the 157th New York is assailed by four regiments belonging to Brig. Gen. George P. Doles.

Doles shifts one regiment, the 12th Georgia, from the left of his brigade to the right, allowing it to fire into the 157th's flank. The New York regiment loses 193 of 409 men before retreating.

4. 3.00–3.15 p.m. Alerted by the arrival of Doles's brigade, Brig. Gen. Francis C. Barlow advances his 1st Division to Blocher's Knoll. He deploys three regiments as skirmishers. He places three regiments and four artillery pieces atop the knoll, keeping two regiments and two more artillery pieces in reserve.

5. 3.15–3.30 p.m. On the northeast side of Rock Creek, the vanguard of Maj. Gen. Jubal Early's division arrives via the Harrisburg Road. Early's artillery commander, Lieut. Col. Hilary Jones, deploys sixteen guns on the east side of the road. Jones's gunners fire into Barlow's infantry, holding them in place.

6. 3.30–3.45 p.m. Five regiments from Brig. Gen. John Gordon's brigade form on the Daniel Bringman farm. (Gordon's sixth regiment protects Jones's artillery.) They advance across Rock Creek, driving back Barlow's skirmishers. After crossing the creek, Gordon's men assault Barlow's infantry regiments atop the knoll.

7. 3.45–4.00 p.m. As Barlow's position crumbles under the pressure of Gordon's attack, Maj. Gen. Carl Schurz (the acting commander of the 11th Corps) dispatches Col. Włodzimierz Krzyżanowski's brigade to Barlow's assistance. Only minutes after getting into position on Barlow's left, Krzyżanowski's men are assailed from two directions—by Doles's men from the north and by Gordon's men from the northeast. Krzyżanowski's brigade loses forty percent of its number and runs off the field.

8. 4.00–4.10 p.m. The remainder of the 1st Division routs, abandoning Blocher's Knoll. Brig. Gen. Barlow falls wounded while trying to direct his men. He is left behind and falls into Confederate hands.

9. 4.10 p.m. Unable to blunt the Confederate attack, Howard sends orders to Schurz, instructing him to fall back abandoning the position north of town. All remaining 3rd Division soldiers withdraw.

Brig. Gen. John B. Gordon commanded the Georgia brigade that bore the brunt of the fighting at Blocher's knoll. His troops attacked from the woods along Rock Creek, losing about 500 officers and men. Gordon's attack caused the Union position to unravel. (NARA)

misunderstood them, or both. In any event, before Barlow's men could be recalled to a safer position, Confederate artillery opened on them. At that point, Barlow's men had to defend the knoll, like it or not. Schurz's only decision of consequence involved sending one brigade—Col. Włodzimierz Krzyżanowski's—to Barlow's assistance, shortly before his troops were overrun.

Barlow's position atop Blocher's knoll was, indeed, untenable, but not so much because of how far out it was. More problematically, the position atop the knoll limited his line of sight. A thicket of trees traced the path of Rock Creek, a waterway that divided the David Blocher and Josiah Benner farmsteads. The trees along the bank prevented Barlow from seeing the buildup of Confederate troops along the Harrisburg Road.

This accumulation of Confederate troops would have concerned Barlow, had he seen it happening. Maj. Gen. Jubal Early's division quietly formed a line of battle on the north side of Rock Creek. At that moment, Early had three brigades of infantry and one artillery battalion, 4,642 officers and men between them, almost double Barlow's contingent. Strangely, none of Col. Devin's exhausted cavalrymen, who were then retiring along the Harrisburg Road, stopped to warn Barlow about this threat.

As Early's infantry prepared for an assault, Lieut. Col. Hilary P. Jones's artillery battalion unlimbered and shelled Barlow's line. The shelling was ferocious. Jones had sixteen guns, and Barlow's supporting battery had only four on the knoll. With no cover, Barlow's infantry had to endure the barrage. In the 17th Connecticut, Lieut. Col. Douglas Fowler tried to calm his skittish men by joking, "Beware of the big ones, boys; the little ones will take care of themselves." Not long after uttering these words, an exploding shell tore out a piece of his head, killing him instantly.

At 3.30 p.m., Confederate infantry joined the attack against the 11th Corps, with two brigades making the initial assault. These belonged to Brig. Gen. George Doles (from Rodes's division) and Brig. Gen. John B. Gordon (from Early's division). Rolling across the Blocher and Benner farm fields, they lurched into the 11th Corps line. In ten or fifteen minutes, Barlow's men gave way, hit from two directions simultaneously. As Barlow bitterly remembered it, the Confederates had "hardly attacked us before my men began to run. No fight at all was made." Barlow's low opinion of his troops was surely callous, but his estimation of the situation was quite accurate, at least when it came to a few regiments. The 68th New York, a unit of 230 officers and men, retreated from the skirmish line after losing only thirteen killed. It did not rally and it lost sixty-seven men missing or captured during the retreat through town. A Georgia soldier later confirmed that the 11th Corps troops were not only defeated, "but stampeded." A few 11th Corps soldiers even admitted that their defense of the knoll was embarrassingly inadequate. A Connecticut soldier claimed that after a few volleys, "Affairs took a Chancellorsville hue ... every man for himself."

Some of Barlow's regiments—the 75th Ohio and 153rd Pennsylvania, in particular—fought well and tried to hold on against fearful odds. In the end, Barlow's two brigades lost fifty-seven percent of their combat strength. Although some of these were lost the next day at Cemetery Hill, most had been felled by the fast-paced action at Blocher's Knoll. Barlow himself was among the wounded. As he rode among his troops, trying to get them to stand fast, a musket ball struck him in the left side, halfway between his armpit and thigh. Unable to remain mounted, he tried to walk, but soon collapsed from loss of blood. Left behind by his retreating troops, he fell into Confederate hands. His captors considered his wound so dangerous that they decided to leave him when the Army of Northern Virginia retreated on July 4. Amazingly, Barlow recovered from his wound and returned to duty in 1864.

After dealing with Barlow's troops, Doles's and Gordon's Georgians turned against Krzyżanowski's men, who occupied an open field at the southwestern foot of the knoll. For ten minutes, the two sides blazed away at each other at 100 yards. A staff officer attached to Krzyżanowski's brigade described the scene vividly:

> Every five or six seconds some poor fellow would throw up his arms with an "Ugh!" and drop; then pick himself up, perhaps, and start for the rear. Another would drop flat on his face, or his back, without a sound; another would break down, and fall together in a heap. Still another would let drop his gun, and holding his shattered arm, would leave the ranks; or, perhaps, stay by to encourage his comrades. One brave boy near me, I remember, shot in the leg, sat there loading and firing with as much regularity and coolness as if untouched, now and then shouting to some comrade in front of him to make room for his shot; while some scared booby, with a scratch scarce deep enough to draw the blood, would run bellowing out of range; or some man, who had completely lost his head in the excitement, though mechanically keeping his place in the line, would load his musket and deliberately fire in the air.

At Gettysburg, Lieut. Col. David R. E. Winn commanded the 4th Georgia. During the attack against Blocher's knoll, Winn was killed by a gunshot wound. His soldiers hastily buried him on the David Blocher farm and left his body there after the Army of Northern Virginia retreated. After the war, Blocher demanded that Winn's family pay for the body's removal, but the family refused. In 1871, Blocher exhumed the corpse and sent it to Georgia, but he removed Winn's gold teeth, holding them for ransom. (*History of the Doles-Cook Brigade of Northern Virginia, C.S.A.*, 1903)

Under heavy fire, Krzyżanowski's brigade crumbled, losing more than forty percent of its 1,420 men. Four of Krzyżanowski's five regimental commanders fell killed or wounded. Those from the brigade who were not killed, wounded, or captured ran off the field.

By 4 p.m., the whole 11th Corps line was crumbling, and Doubleday was pleading with Howard for reinforcements. Schurz, who commanded the 11th Corps, informed Howard that he could spare no additional troops. Even before the fighting started, Schurz had pleaded with Howard to release one of the two reserve brigades on Cemetery Hill to the north side of town, but Howard denied each request. Initially, Howard directed Doubleday to hold on a while longer and await the arrival of Maj. Gen. Henry Slocum's 12th Corps, which, so far as Howard knew, was making its way to Gettysburg from the vicinity of Littlestown, Pennsylvania. These reinforcements, Howard believed, would relieve the pressure.

However, the collapse of Barlow's division changed his mind. At 4.10 p.m., when Howard realized how dire the situation had grown, he sent orders to Schurz and Doubleday, instructing them to fall back gradually, "disputing every inch of ground." Both corps, Howard demanded, had to pass through Gettysburg and reform atop Cemetery Hill, where Howard had posted his only reserve unit, Brig. Gen. Adolph von Steinwehr's 2nd Division, 11th Corps.

One by one, each Union unit made haste to the rally point. Within the next ten minutes, Robinson's 1st Corps division pulled off Oak

RETREAT FROM BLOCHER'S KNOLL, 3.30–4.00 P.M. (PP. 70–71)

The most important tactical action of July 1 involved the collapse of the 1st Division, 11th Corps, at 3.30 p.m. This fight took place on the fields of the David Blocher farm, a twenty-three acre property located along the Carlisle Road. The only appreciable rise in ground in this area was Blocher's Knoll, a hillock that stood southwest of Rock Creek. Thick woods (**1**) skirted the banks of the creek, which ran north–south through this sector of the field.

At approximately 2.00 p.m., Brig. Gen. Francis C. Barlow's division took position atop the knoll, hoping to get into a position to deal with the threat posed by Maj. Gen. Robert Rodes's division on Oak Hill. Barlow faced two of his regiments—the 107th Ohio and 25th Ohio—to the northwest and one regiment—the 153rd Pennsylvania—to the northeast. Two other units—the 75th Ohio and a battalion from the 17th Connecticut—took position in reserve, hidden behind the knoll's crest. Finally, four guns belonging to Battery G, 4th U.S. Light Artillery, held a position atop the knoll's highest point, immediately behind the 25th Ohio.

Sometime after 3.00 p.m., Confederate infantry commenced its attack on Barlow's division. Brig. George P. Doles's brigade from Rodes's division moved first, followed by Brig. Gen. John B. Gordon's brigade of Maj. Gen. Jubal Early's division. Near the intersection of the Carlisle and Table Rock roads, Doles's brigade became embroiled in a fight with the 157th New York from Brig. Gen. Alexander Schimmelfennig's division and Doles's men had to pause to deal with it. Moving ahead without Doles's support, Gordon's brigade drove back Barlow's skirmishers, crossed Rock Creek, and ascended the northeast slope of the knoll. As Gordon's men cleared the woods, the two sides opened fire.

Barlow's men took the worst of the punishment. Pvt. Reuben Ruch of the 153rd Pennsylvania recalled how the dead "were piled up in every shape, some on their backs, some on their faces, and others turned and twisted in every imaginable shape … As I stood between those two lines of battle, viewing the windrow of human dead composed of my old comrades, it presented a picture which will never fade from my memory while I remain on earth—a picture which tongue cannot tell nor pen describe."

At the height of the emergency, Barlow moved the 75th Ohio and the battalion from the 17th Connecticut to the crest to shore up his right flank. Meanwhile, Schimmelfenning sent Col. Włodzimierz Krzyżanowski's brigade to support Barlow's left flank. But these reinforcements did little good. With Gordon's Georgians pressing vigorously and with the reappearance of Doles's men, Barlow's line broke. The 13th and 60th Georgia crested the knoll's highest point and began firing into the Union soldiers who had been driven back into the low ground. With disintegrating infantry support and having lost their commander, Lieut. Bayard Wilkeson, the gunners of Battery G limbered up and galloped off the field (**2**). In addition to Wilkeson, Battery G lost one man killed, twelve horses killed, five men wounded, and four men captured (**3**).

Eager to get away, many of Barlow's infantry abandoned their equipment and weapons along the slope, making themselves more fleet of foot. Barlow tried to quell the alarm (**4**), riding among his men to rally them, but a Confederate ball pierced his left side, forcing him to dismount. Two helpful soldiers carried him under each arm, until they, too, got swept up in the rout. They dropped Barlow (**5**) in the grass and he soon fell into enemy hands.

This photograph depicts ten company officers from the 153rd Pennsylvania, a nine-month regiment that belonged to Barlow's division. This regiment was scheduled to muster out of service in three weeks. Just prior to battle, the regimental commander, Maj. John Freauff, addressed his men and told them that if any wished to step out of ranks and avoid battle, he would allow it. But none of them did so. At Gettysburg, the 153rd Pennsylvania suffered a loss of 211 out of 497 officers and men. (Northampton County Historical and Genealogical Society/National Park Service)

Ridge, sacrificing the 16th Maine to make its getaway. Meanwhile, Col. George von Amsberg's brigade of the 11th Corps evacuated the fields north of Gettysburg, with Doles's Georgians hot on their heels. Although several 11th Corps artillery batteries attempted to cover the retreat with a heavy barrage, the withdrawal of Amsberg's men was far from organized. His regiments broke up as they entered alleyways and cross streets, colliding with Barlow's shattered division, now commanded by Brig. Gen. Adelbert Ames. More than any emotion, panic infected the 11th Corps. As he ran for his life along Carlisle Street, Pvt. James M. Bailey of the 17th Connecticut remembered, "Men and officers of a dozen different commands were flocking up the street, shrieking out names of their regiments, commanding and countermanding. Frightened horses, swearing drivers, ambitious patriots, crazy citizens, and the deuce only knows what, a conglomeration of all that was devilish, Babelish and skittish." No one could deny that this was a rout.

The two Georgia brigades that had dislodged the 11th Corps so effectively—Doles's and Gordon's—suffered heavily for their success. Doles's brigade had lost more than 200 men, about sixteen percent of its strength, while Gordon's suffered more than 500, almost thirty percent. Deluged with prisoners and wounded men from both sides, each brigade received orders to halt as soon as it entered the borough's outskirts. Doles directed his brigade to rejoin Rodes's division near Pennsylvania College, while Early replaced Gordon's men with two fresh units, Brig. Gen. Harry Hays's Louisiana brigade and Col. Isaac Avery's North Carolina brigade, 2,539 officers and men between them. There was still enough daylight left for another attack. At the time, it seemed possible that these two brigades could deliver the *coup de grâce*.

SEMINARY RIDGE

At 4 p.m., the Union line was coming apart. Under an aggressive attack from Heth's division, the three brigades that defended McPherson's Ridge—Dana's, Meredith's, and Biddle's—had to withdraw. Then, under pressure from Rodes's division, Doubleday wisely ordered Robinson's division to withdraw from Oak Ridge, as well. "It was evident Lee's whole army was

A fierce leader with a disregard for danger, Maj. Gen. William Dorsey Pender commanded the infantry division that made the final attack against the 1st Corps at the Lutheran Seminary. In a stunning charge, Pender's Division drove the 1st Corps off the ridge. The next day, Pender was mortally wounded by a stray artillery shell. He died on July 18 during the retreat through the Shenandoah Valley. (Library of Congress)

approaching," Doubleday later reported. "Our tired troops had been fighting desperately, some of them for six hours. They were thoroughly exhausted, and General Howard had no re-enforcements to give me." Doubleday issued orders, instructing all cohesive regiments to fall back to Seminary Ridge and establish a new line at the edge of town.

Of course, despite Doubleday's hyperbole, Lee's *entire* army was not approaching at that exact moment, only Brig. Gen. Pender's division. During the morning march toward Gettysburg, Pender's men had been following behind Heth's. When Heth's division made its attack in the afternoon, Pender had given his brigade commanders orders to pass through Heth's line if it halted. At 4 p.m., that eventuality occurred. Not only had Heth's men been badly mauled by their assault, but Heth had been knocked unconscious by a piece of shell or musket ball. Although he recovered from his wound, for the remainder of the battle, command of his division fell to his senior brigade commander, Pettigrew.

Pender's division formed atop McPherson's Ridge, passing through Pettigrew's shattered lines. Col. Abner Perrin's South Carolina brigade held the right flank and Brig. Gen. Alfred Scales's North Carolina brigade held the left. Brig. Gen. James Lane's North Carolina brigade veered off to the south, following on the heels of one of Buford's mounted regiments, going beyond the Fairfield Road, probably much farther away than where Pender intended. And finally, under orders from Hill, Pender held Brig. Gen. Edward L. Thomas's Georgia brigade in reserve. For various reasons, Pender had only about 2,860 soldiers to contribute toward the final push.

Doubleday's men did not intend to stay on Seminary Ridge for long. At 4.10 p.m., Howard's instructions to "fall back gradually" arrived, giving the 1st Corps troops license to retreat. Unfortunately, Doubleday's men could not simply quit the field. The area around the Lutheran Seminary had been turned into a vast field hospital, and all the wounded needed to be evacuated. Doubleday reckoned that the 1st Corps had brought 9,800 soldiers onto the field, but now, perhaps as many as 5,000 were in need of medical assistance. The artillery needed time to limber up and the ambulance crews needed time to load their sufferers. In short, the men who could still stand and shoot needed to buy time for their wounded comrades to escape.

In a few frantic minutes, the 1st Corps troops cobbled together a new line. Col. Theodore Gates's brigade (formerly Chapman Biddle's) held the left end of the line. It formed between the Seminary buildings and the Fairfield Road. The Iron Brigade (now under Col. Robinson) extended that line northward, connecting with Dana's brigade, whose right flank stopped at the Chambersburg Pike. Cutler's brigade (with the 6th Wisconsin attached) extended Dana's line northward from the inner railroad cut to the McPherson woodlot, which marked the south end of Oak Ridge. With Robinson's division now withdrawing, these men now held the right of the 1st Corps.

The new line along Seminary Ridge had several advantages. First, in front of the Seminary Buildings, the 1st Corps possessed the barricade of furniture and fence rails constructed earlier in the day by Robinson's division. In addition to the thick grove of trees, the barricade provided much needed concealment from Confederate artillery. Second, the entire ridgeline—from the Fairfield Road to the inner cut—was covered by Union artillery. During the course of the withdrawal from McPherson's Ridge, the 1st Corps artillery

This image was one of two taken by Alexander Gardner on July 5 or 6, 1863, depicting the corpses of Union soldiers who had been killed at Gettysburg. The exact location of this photograph is unknown; however, current theories suggest that these bodies belonged to 1st Corps troops killed on July 1. (Library of Congress)

commander, Col. Charles Wainwright, had assembled twenty-two cannon to watch the open ground east of McPherson's Ridge. If the Confederates advanced into the open, they were sure to take heavy losses from these well-placed Union guns. Finally, Col. William Gamble's cavalry brigade (and Brig. Gen. Buford with it) lent assistance. These Union cavalry troopers took shelter behind stone walls, extending the left end of the 1st Corps from Schultz Woods to the vicinity of the David McMillan farm. With Gamble's men in place, the left flank of the corps could not be easily turned.

The advance of Scales's and Perrin's brigades was anything but tidy. As they exited the woods and descended the east slope of McPherson's Ridge, the 1st Corps artillery opened tremendous holes in their line. Scales reported, "Here the brigade encountered a most terrific fire of grape and shell on our flank, and grape and musketry in our front. Every discharge made sad havoc in our line." Scales himself was among the first casualties. A shell fragment struck him in the leg and he turned over command to Lieut. Col. George T. Gordon, a former British officer who now served with the Confederacy.

The Federal artillery effectively destroyed Scales's brigade, pinning down the survivors in the low ground in front of Seminary Ridge. But the rebels could smell victory in the air. The 1st Corps troops were few in number, low on ammunition, and exhausted—and the Confederates knew it. Many 1st Corps regiments mustered only enough men to form a single company. Powder-grimed, sweaty, drained, and shell-shocked, they lacked water. Further, some regiments no longer possessed their commanders, with the second- or third-in-command directing the survivors. Yet, the bluecoats vowed to fight on, as one Pennsylvanian wrote, "to prevent what was an orderly retreat from becoming a rout." Years later, a 1st Corps staff officer, Lieut. Joseph J. Rosengarten, remembered the last stand at the Lutheran Seminary as "something worthy of high praise." In his opinion, those regiments that stood and fired away their last rounds at Pender's advancing tide showed steadiness that "could not be surpassed."

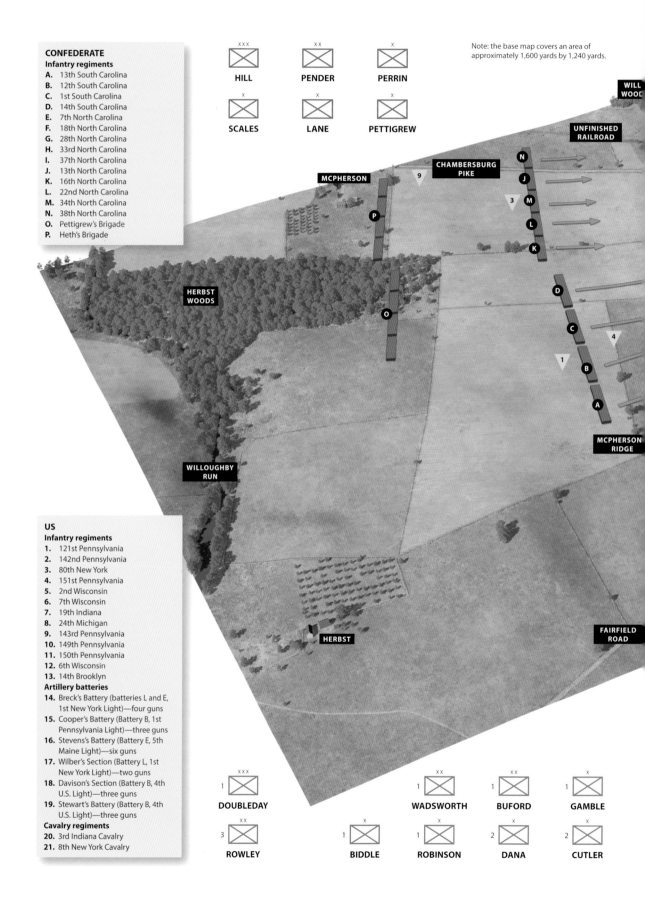

CONFEDERATE
Infantry regiments
A. 13th South Carolina
B. 12th South Carolina
C. 1st South Carolina
D. 14th South Carolina
E. 7th North Carolina
F. 18th North Carolina
G. 28th North Carolina
H. 33rd North Carolina
I. 37th North Carolina
J. 13th North Carolina
K. 16th North Carolina
L. 22nd North Carolina
M. 34th North Carolina
N. 38th North Carolina
O. Pettigrew's Brigade
P. Heth's Brigade

HILL
PENDER
PERRIN
SCALES
LANE
PETTIGREW

Note: the base map covers an area of
approximately 1,600 yards by 1,240 yards.

WILL
WOOD

UNFINISHED
RAILROAD

CHAMBERSBURG
PIKE

MCPHERSON

HERBST
WOODS

MCPHERSON
RIDGE

WILLOUGHBY
RUN

HERBST

FAIRFIELD
ROAD

US
Infantry regiments
1. 121st Pennsylvania
2. 142nd Pennsylvania
3. 80th New York
4. 151st Pennsylvania
5. 2nd Wisconsin
6. 7th Wisconsin
7. 19th Indiana
8. 24th Michigan
9. 143rd Pennsylvania
10. 149th Pennsylvania
11. 150th Pennsylvania
12. 6th Wisconsin
13. 14th Brooklyn
Artillery batteries
14. Breck's Battery (batteries L and E,
    1st New York Light)—four guns
15. Cooper's Battery (Battery B, 1st
    Pennsylvania Light)—three guns
16. Stevens's Battery (Battery E, 5th
    Maine Light)—six guns
17. Wilber's Section (Battery L, 1st
    New York Light)—two guns
18. Davison's Section (Battery B, 4th
    U.S. Light)—three guns
19. Stewart's Battery (Battery B, 4th
    U.S. Light)—three guns
Cavalry regiments
20. 3rd Indiana Cavalry
21. 8th New York Cavalry

DOUBLEDAY
ROWLEY
WADSWORTH
BUFORD
GAMBLE
BIDDLE
ROBINSON
DANA
CUTLER

JULY 1: PENDER'S ASSAULT

In the late afternoon, Lieut. Gen. A. P. Hill committed a fresh division—Maj. Gen. William Dorsey Pender's—to the assault on the sector held by Maj. Gen. Abner Doubleday's 1st Corps. Doubleday's men covered the northern portion of Seminary Ridge, guarding the roads that entered Gettysburg from the west. The bluecoats hoped to buy time so the routed elements of the 11th Corps could escape to the south side of town. Eager to deliver a killing blow, Pender's men charged from McPherson's Ridge, under heavy cannon and small arms fire as they crossed the deadly ground. After thirty desperate minutes of fighting, the Confederates took possession of Seminary Ridge, but at heavy cost.

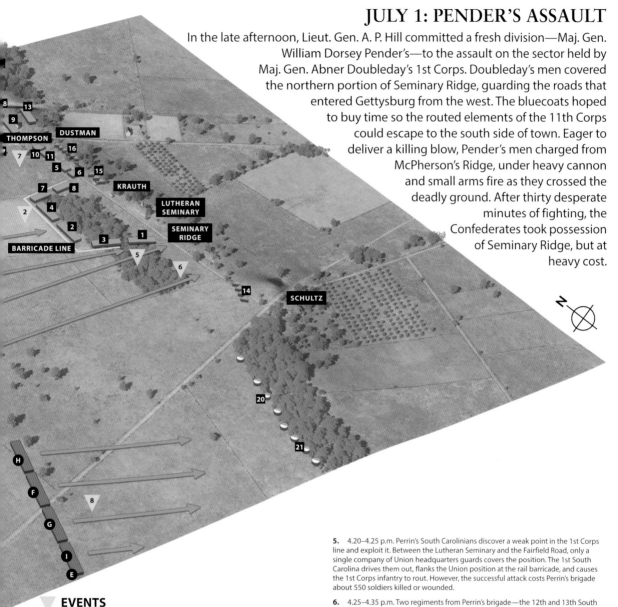

▼ EVENTS

(Times are approximate.)

1. 4.00–4.05 p.m. Lieut. Gen. Hill issues orders to Pender, instructing him to charge the enemy position at Seminary Ridge. Three of Pender's brigades—Scales's, Perrin's, and Lane's—carry out the order.

2. 4.10 p.m. Maj. Gen. Doubleday receives orders from the wing commander, Maj. Gen. Oliver Howard, to fall back gradually. But with Pender's soldiers forming for attack in front of them, many of the individual 1st Corps units choose to hold the Seminary Ridge position for as long as possible, until the wounded and artillery can be evacuated. In front of the Seminary, the Union infantrymen take shelter behind a barricade of fence rails.

3. 4.10–4.20 p.m. Brig. Gen. Alfred Scales's brigade of Pender's division attacks the north end of Doubleday's line. It is stopped cold by well-aimed Union artillery fire. Caught in the open, Scales's men go to ground in the open fields west of Seminary Ridge. Out of 1,400 officers and men, Scales's brigade loses 545 killed or wounded, including Scales himself, who is wounded in the leg.

4. 4.15–4.20 p.m. At the south end of Doubleday's line, Brig. Gen. Abner Perrin's South Carolinians advance unflinchingly through heavy artillery fire. A Union artillery officer who is impressed by their determination later writes, "Lee may well be proud of his infantry."

5. 4.20–4.25 p.m. Perrin's South Carolinians discover a weak point in the 1st Corps line and exploit it. Between the Lutheran Seminary and the Fairfield Road, only a single company of Union headquarters guards covers the position. The 1st South Carolina drives them out, flanks the Union position at the rail barricade, and causes the 1st Corps infantry to rout. However, the successful attack costs Perrin's brigade about 550 soldiers killed or wounded.

6. 4.25–4.35 p.m. Two regiments from Perrin's brigade—the 12th and 13th South Carolina—drive off several squadrons of Brig. Gen. William Gamble's brigade (belonging to the 3rd Indiana Cavalry and 8th New York Cavalry) from their positions near the Fairfield Road. Afterwards, Perrin's two regiments turn east and participate in the pursuit of routed Union forces through the town.

7. 4.30 p.m. Just north of the Seminary, the 1st and 14th South Carolina attack a section of Union artillery commanded by Lieut. Benjamin Wilber. The South Carolinians kill seven of Wilber's horses and two of his men, forcing Wilber to abandon one of his guns, a three-inch ordnance rifle. The South Carolinians capture the gun in triumph.

8. 4.35–4.50: Arriving late, Brig. Gen. James H. Lane's North Carolina brigade forms on the right of Pender's division with orders to support the breakthrough. South of the Fairfield Road, Lane's troops encounter organized elements from Gamble's cavalry brigade. Lane's men halt and Lane detaches one regiment, sending it forward as skirmishers. After dealing with Gamble's troopers and losing time, Lane advances the remainder of his brigade onto the David McMillan farm atop Seminary Ridge. Under orders from Pender, Lane halts for the evening.

9. 5.15 p.m. As Union forces retreat to Cemetery Hill, Gen. Robert E. Lee arrives via the Chambersburg Pike. He and his staff establish headquarters adjacent to the Mary Thompson House.

10. 5.30 p.m. Lieut. Gen. James Longstreet arrives at the Thompson house to confer with Lee. They debate their options.

This photograph depicts the east slope of Seminary Ridge with the Lutheran Theological Seminary sitting prominently atop its crest. During the afternoon, soldiers from the 1st Corps mounted a heroic final stand in front of the Seminary Buildings, even piling rails and furniture to create an impromptu breastwork. But in the end, Pender's charge dislodged them and the ambulatory soldiers retreated down the slope (in the foreground) and headed into the town. (Library of Congress)

Eighteen-year-old First Lieutenant Andrew Gregg Tucker of the 142nd Pennsylvania was wounded during the final stand of the 1st Corps at the Lutheran Seminary. Kept as a patient in the Seminary's field hospital, he died of his wounds on July 5. Another soldier from the 142nd Pennsylvania recalled the sight of Tucker's burial on the Seminary's grounds: "I could see into the garden, they were holding the body over the grave when the head slipped over the edge of the blanket and the Lieutenant's beautiful jet black hair dragged over the ground." Tucker's body was later exhumed and reburied in Lewisburg Cemetery in Union County, Pennsylvania. (Seminary Museum and Education Center, Gettysburg/ US Military History Institute)

Rosengarten's praise was warranted, but in the end, the last stand of the 1st Corps proved insufficient to stop Pender's advance. The weak link was the area between the barricade and the Fairfield Road, which was held by only one infantry company. Perrin discovered this soft spot and infiltrated it with the 1st South Carolina. That regiment enfiladed the barricade line, unhinging the whole defense. Maj. Alexander Biddle, commander of the 121st Pennsylvania, was in the middle of this maelstrom. He wrote, "Bullets were striking everywhere and men [were] falling … A man receiv[ed] a wound almost every moment and the noise of Artillery shots in the houses and the smack of a ball against wood work [were] occurring every moment." In the chaos, Maj. Biddle found his cousin, Chapman, on the steps of the Seminary. Although wounded, Col. Biddle resumed command of the brigade, taking back his horse that Maj. Biddle had rounded up and mounted. The swirling battle seemed not to end.

South of the Fairfield Road, Buford's dismounted troopers inflicted heavy losses on the 12th and 13th South Carolina, but in the end, the rebels managed to drive off the Union cavalry. This was the hardest fighting that involved Buford's cavalry and probably where Gamble's brigade suffered the bulk of its ninety-nine losses.

One by one, each regiment chose to leave the field and fall back through the borough. Not every unit escaped cleanly. For instance, soldiers from Perrin's brigade caught one of the last batteries to evacuate, Lieut. Benjamin W. Wilber's section of Battery L, 1st New York Light Artillery. The South Carolinians trapped the last gun by wounding one of the wheel horses. Swiftly, Lieut. Wilber unhitched the wounded animal, but then came a volley, killing the five remaining horses and also the horse that Wilber was riding. One ball passed through Wilber's coat and another through his whiskers, but somehow, he remained unhurt. Realizing he must abandon his gun or lose his whole command, Wilber shouted to his men to "save themselves if they could." As the New York gunners scattered down the east slope of Seminary Ridge, Perrin's soldiers claimed the abandoned cannon. In the end, Battery L lost only two men killed, but its equine contingent paid severely. Twenty-two horses were killed or maimed by the fighting.

By 4.30 p.m., the Lutheran Seminary was in Confederate hands.

THE RETREAT THROUGH TOWN

The Union retreat began at 4.10 p.m. From Oak Ridge, the weary columns of Robinson's division made their way south along two of the borough's main thoroughfares: Washington Street and Baltimore Street. By 4.20 p.m., the 11th Corps line had collapsed, increasing the number of retreating Union troops and adding to the retreat's disorganization. Frightened soldiers ran everywhere. They coursed through side streets and alleyways. Some clambered over fences and into backyards, the fleetest of foot making haste to outrun their pursuers.

For the people of Gettysburg, the sight of the retreating Union army was never to be forgotten. Teenager Albertus McCreary first heard the commotion from his family's dinner table, and with his folks, he stood on the porch, handing out water to parched soldiers as they streamed to the rear. Decades later McCreary recollected, "The street was full of Union soldiers, running and pushing each other, sweaty and black from powder and dust."

Gettysburg's citizens were unprepared for the tumult. When the army occupied the farmsteads north and west of town, staff officers advised the occupants to seek shelter with neighbors. Not expecting a mass retreat, they did not issue similar directives to the citizens who lived in town. Further, the borough lacked civilian leadership. The burgess had fled on June 26, shortly before the arrival of Early's division. The exact number who stayed is unknown, but at this juncture, Union officers frantically

This image, taken on July 15, 1863, depicts the area east of Seminary Ridge. During the retreat, the roads (Springs Avenue in the foreground and Middle Street off to the right) would have been choked with panicked 1st Corps soldiers. (Library of Congress)

The Union retreat through Gettysburg town, *c.* 4.10–4.45 p.m.

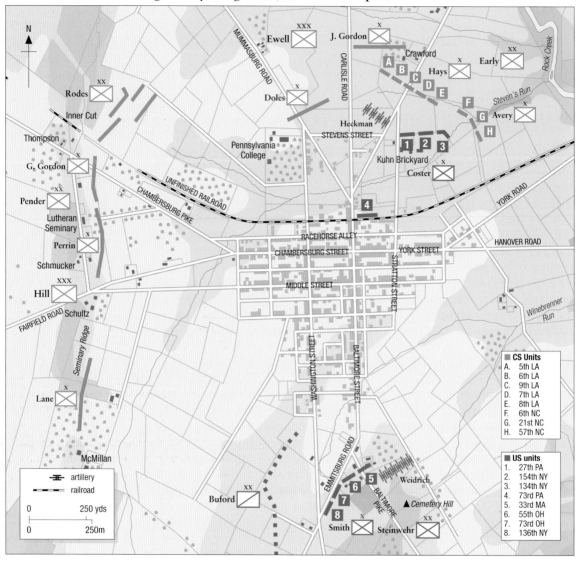

tried to get them out of harm's way. A mounted officer told the McCreary family to go inside: "All you good people go down into your cellars or you will all be killed." Hardly had the family obeyed when a Union soldier came crashing through the backyard, with Confederates hot on his heels. A rebel cried out, "Shoot that fellow going over the fence!" Peering from a small window in the cellar, Albertus McCreary tried to get a glimpse of the invaders. He recalled, "There was more and more shooting, until the sound was one continuous racket." The borough had now become part of the battlefield.

To save the town, the 11th Corps still had one card left to play, Brig. Gen. Steinwehr's division. Ever since 2 p.m., it sat atop the north side of Cemetery Hill, improving its position by toppling fence rails and digging artillery lunettes. When Ewell's Confederates struck Barlow's division at 3.30 p.m., Schurz sent a request for reinforcements, hoping that a fresh brigade from Steinwehr's division might launch a counterattack and save the embattled position at Blocher's Knoll. Howard denied Schurz's initial request. He believed Steinwehr needed to have a sufficient number of troops to hold Cemetery Hill in case the line was overrun. When Barlow's situation deteriorated, Schurz repeated his request. With that, Howard acquiesced. He sent a message to Steinwehr, instructing him to detach a brigade and rush it to Schurz's assistance. Accordingly, Col. Charles Coster's men got the call. They shouldered their rifles and hurried to the threatened spot.

At about 4.30 p.m., Coster met Schurz along Baltimore Street. Together, they discussed the deployment of the brigade. Coster detached one regiment—the 73rd Pennsylvania—and placed it near the railroad depot on Carlisle Street. Meanwhile, Coster marched his other three regiments—the 27th Pennsylvania, the 134th New York, and the 154th New York—along Stratton Street and then turned them east on Stevens Street. The brigade came to a halt where Stevens Street dead-ended. This was a brickyard owned by John P. Kuhn. Coster's men faced north, where a large, sloping wheatfield confronted them. Meanwhile, a battery of Ohio artillery took position on the brigade's left flank, one block north, and along the Harrisburg Road. Resting their rifles on a fence, Coster's men could barely see anything in their front. A thick blanket of smoke covered the rolling fields north of Gettysburg. They could not see two fresh enemy brigades from Early's division coming straight at them.

Including the nearby artillery, Coster had only 1,030 men. Meanwhile, Early's brigades consisted of at least 2,500. Schurz had hoped Coster might counterattack and retake Blocher's Knoll. Ten minutes ago, so Schurz supposed, that might have been possible. But now, he wrote, it was entirely "too late for executing the offensive movement upon the enemy's left flank, which I had originally contemplated." More problematically, Coster's position was not ideal. The slope in front of the brigade narrowed its field of fire. Had time allowed, Coster might have repositioned his troops, but before any of his regiments were fully aligned, the Confederates appeared out of the smoke, about sixty yards distant. Unable to do anything else, Coster's men opened fire.

The results were predictable. Early's brigades overlapped Coster's position, or as one New York officer put it, "we were handsomely flanked." The volume of fire overwhelmed the Union troops such that they could only retreat, surrender, or die. Most chose to run for it, and the brigade attempted a frenzied withdrawal. Unfortunately, most of Coster's men could not merely turn and run. Instead, they had to back out of the alleyway. They bolted west, toward the lane's opening, and then turned south down Stratton Street. In a few minutes, Brig. Gen. Harry Hays's Louisiana brigade choked off this crucial intersection. Some of Coster's men—those who were still in the lane—had to fight their way out at close quarters. Adjt. Alanson Crosby of the 154th New York wrote, "The only avenue of retreat lay through a road, along which a rebel column was dashing, in persuit [sic] of our troops that had fallen back on the left of us. We entered the road, and a fierce hand to hand conflict ensued. The opposing forces were mingled in promiscous [sic] confusion. Four color-bearers in the 154th were shot down in rapid succession. The only resource left was to cut through the enemy's ranks. The bayonet was used, but alas, what could a mere handful of men do against

Colonel Charles Coster commanded the 1st Brigade, 2nd Division, 11th Corps. Late in the day, he received orders to reinforce the embattled position at Blocher's Knoll. Before he could get his troops to that location, Coster was attacked at the Kuhn Brickyard at the northeast corner of the town. Overwhelmed by two Confederate brigades, Coster's brigade lost 563 officers and men, including 313 taken prisoner. (US Army Military History Institute)

German-born Maj. Gen Carl Schurz commanded the 11th Corps on July 1. It fell to him to keep the retreat as orderly as possible. After the battle, he reported that "the streets [were] filled with vehicles of every description and overrun with men of the First Corps." Schurz survived the battle without injury, and on July 2, when Maj. Gen. Howard resumed corps command, Schurz reverted to command of the 3rd Division, 11th Corps. (Library of Congress)

the thousands that surrounded us on all sides?" Crosby was among 178 of his regiment who surrendered.

Coster's three regiments lost 563 officers and men, including 313 prisoners. Yet, these casualties did not tell the whole story. The fight at the brickyard so disoriented the unwounded survivors that many could not make it back to the rally point atop Cemetery Hill. For instance, the 154th New York took 239 officers and men into the July 1 action, but only fifteen men and three officers managed to reassemble that evening. At dusk, Maj. Lewis D. Warner of that regiment arrived with fifty-two additional soldiers who had been on detached duty (and had thus missed the first day of the battle). Warner asked Schurz where he might find the 154th New York. Schurz snarled, "There is no such regiment! It is all used up!" Warner recollected, "All the information I could obtain was vague and unsatisfactory. At length I found Col. Coster, commanding [the] Brigade, who informed me that the Brigade had suffered severely." Deeply mortified by this news, Warner asked the survivors about the brickyard fight. He concluded, "Of the generalship displayed in sending our little Brigade out a mile from any support without knowing what they were to meet, it is not my province to judge, and this is more particularly the case, as being absent on duty, I have only hearsay evidence … One thing is sure, it was no fault of the men that the regiment is thus almost annihilated."

As Coster's brigade dissolved, a more successful holding action occurred on the other Union flank, near McMillan Woods. There, a contingent from Col. Gamble's cavalry brigade (from Buford's division) made a valiant stand against Pender's division. Gamble had only a handful of troopers available. His command had not suffered heavily during the morning skirmish, but so many men had exhausted their horses or shot away their ammunition that their line was a hollow mockery of what it had been. Gamble's troopers confronted a sizable foe, Brig. Gen. James H. Lane's brigade, 1,730 aggregate. Lane's North Carolinians had been advancing eastward along the south side of the Fairfield Road, cautiously approaching McMillan's Woods, just beyond the left flank of the 1st Corps.

From behind stone walls and fence rails, Gamble's men fired on Lane's approach. As Lane described it, Gamble's brigade proved so annoying that he ordered his skirmish line reinforced with forty additional men, and then, when Gamble's men still refused to give way, he ordered an assault. As Lane reported, "the men gave a yell, and rushed forward at the double-quick." Before Lane's men reached them, Gamble's troopers mounted up and withdrew to the low ground at the western foot of Cemetery Hill. The short skirmish had not been costly for either side; however, it brought an end to Lane's advance. The order to halt came from the division commander, Pender, who did not want his freshest brigade to get into any trouble. Pender told Lane not to move another inch unless Lee sent an order for an army-wide assault. Fearful of the Union artillery that had reassembled atop Cemetery Hill, Lane instructed his men to retire 100 yards into the woods and hunker down for the night.

Elsewhere, the Confederate pursuit ground to a halt. The borough's streets fractured the lines of battle. Confederate soldiers detached themselves from their commands, seeking out prisoners. To some witnesses, the scene formed a frightening tableaux, with blood-drunk, triumphant rebels competing with each other to take the greatest number of captives. One Connecticut soldier who was trapped in the town recalled seeing bands of roving Confederates, bashing in doors: "some were engaged in bringing in prisoners, or bringing them *down*, while up and down, around and about, dashed the mounted infantry, their uncouth rigs, slouched hats with trailing feather forcibly reminding me of pictures of brigand scenes in olden Spain."

Gettysburg civilians did not sit passively as the battle flowed through their town. The most enterprising among them shielded, protected, or hid Union soldiers from capture. Elizabeth Skelly, who lived on Middle Street, threw herself in front of a squad of Confederates who were attempting to drag off a wounded Union lieutenant. She told the Confederates that she would dress the officer's wound first and *then* they could take him. After she gave them a thorough scolding, the enemy soldiers agreed. They departed, but never returned. For the rest of the battle, the Skelly family concealed the wounded officer, returning him to Union authorities on July 4.

Meanwhile, in her home on Baltimore Street, Fannie Buehler sheltered a dozen Union soldiers on July 1—mostly men with minor wounds. Before leaving town, Buehler's husband had hidden all the family's hams, butter, eggs, potatoes, tea, coffee, and sugar in the cellar. Fannie Buehler used these to keep her sufferers well fed. When a squad of Confederates showed up at her door, accusing her of concealing Union soldiers, she snarled, "You are mistaken, sir; there *are* Union soldiers in my house, but none of them are *concealed*." Buehler invited the enemy squad into her home and showed them the wounded men. Disappointed at finding no ambulatory soldiers, the commander vowed to return to Buehler's house with papers to parole them. Much like the squad that stopped by the Skelly house, these Confederates never returned.

Another Baltimore Street resident took a more secretive approach. That night, Catherine Garlach discovered a Union division commander, Brig. Gen. Alexander Schimmelfennig, hiding in her woodshed. Schimmelfennig's horse had been killed during the retreat through town, and to escape pursuing Confederates, he crawled into a drainage ditch that led to Garlach's backyard. Bravely, she kept the general hidden and continued to feed him by taking him bread and water when she went to slop her hogs. Thus, Schimmelfennig remained undetected for the rest of the battle.

Many Union soldiers who quartered inside homes during the retreat required immediate medical attention. Approximately 4,300 Union soldiers had been shot on July 1, and hundreds of these were trapped behind Confederate lines. As Confederate troops began clearing houses, they corralled wounded men and confined them at secure locations. The Lutheran Seminary and the Pennsylvania College Buildings became the principal collection points for the captured wounded. Cpl. George Kimball, a 1st Corps soldier, had been wounded in the groin at Oak Ridge. Confederate soldiers carried him to the President's House Building at Pennsylvania College. There, the Confederate surgeon who examined him told Kimball that his wounds were mortal and that he should prepare for death; however, one citizen, Alice K. Baugher (a music teacher and daughter of the college president), refused to give up on him. Even though the rebels had robbed her family of everything medicinal, Kimball recalled, "This loyal lady ... used every means in her power to woo me back to life." When Robert E. Lee arrived at President's House to observe the battle lines from the upper floor, Baugher gave Lee a withering look, that "left no doubt in my mind," so remembered Kimball, "as to her sympathy with the loyal army and her contempt for rebels. Verily, the boys in blue are not the only heroes of Gettysburg."

The largest buildings inside the borough became makeshift field hospitals. The railroad depot, the express office, the county court house, two hotels, a public school, and seven churches all held dozens of wounded men. Aided by civilian volunteers, captured Union surgeons worked round the clock, while Confederate sentries stood watch over them. Pvt. James Bailey of the 17th Connecticut remembered the grim scenes inside the Trinity German Reformed Church on Stratton Street:

Private James Montgomery Bailey of the 17th Connecticut was captured by Confederate forces during the retreat through town. Caught in an alleyway alongside a comrade, Bailey later remembered the hopelessness of their case: "But I looked in vain, not the slightest opening appeared, and the only alternative left was to lay down our guns, and wait for the unfolding of our destiny." (*Life in Danbury*, Boston, 1873)

There were two tables at which two surgeons were operating ... The pews had been turned into beds, and were now mostly filled with wounded of both sides. Reader, did you ever stand within a Church hospital?—if not, the first time you enter your sanctuary, imagine the pews transformed into bunks, on which the stretched scores of mangled men, writhing, groaning and sobbing with pain, the aisles filled with little pools of blood, and the pulpit, from which you have heard sound the gentle language of the Prince of Peace, covered with diversity of bloody, powder-begrimed weapons, and you will get an idea of my impressions as I looked into the room.

Gettysburgians' private dwellings became hospitals. More than forty private residences in the borough provided shelter during the first day of the battle. Quite often, desperate soldiers forced their way inside. Merciful residents admitted soldiers by dozens, quartering them in bedrooms, shredding their linens to make bandages. Few had any control over who showed up. A New York soldier who lost two toes from an exploding shell simply barged into a house owned by David McMillan at the corner of Chambersburg and Franklin Street. The soldier, Pvt. Richard Laracy, was lured by the sight of a water pump in the backyard. Once inside the house, Laracy discovered fourteen wounded men who had arrived seeking the same pump. By nightfall, five female neighbors arrived to assist the McMillans in caring for all their patients.

CEMETERY HILL

Whether in small groups or as organized commands, Union soldiers began arriving at Cemetery Hill—a large, mostly treeless hill at the south edge of town named for the town's local burial plot, the Evergreen Cemetery. Earlier in the day, Howard had made the decision to use Cemetery Hill as a rallying point. After learning of Reynolds's death, he had headed south from the Fahnestock building and stopped at the hill's highest point to survey the ground. Howard determined that Cemetery Hill was the "only tenable position for my limited force." So Howard reported, the hill "commanded every eminence within easy range." Quite probably, Howard did not concoct the idea to secure Cemetery Hill entirely on his own. Yet, in his postwar writings Howard awarded himself the ample credit for forethought. Forty-four years later, he claimed that he and one of his staff, Col. Theodore Meysenberg, reasoned that the hill would shape the next few days of battle. As Howard wrote, "We sat on our horses, side by side, looking northward, when I said: 'This seems to be a good position, colonel,' and his own prompt and characteristic reply was: 'It is the only position, general.' We both meant *position for Meade's army.*"

Whether genuinely remembered or not, Howard's selection of Cemetery Hill helped stave off disaster. For the retreating Union soldiers, this location was easy to find, and when they arrived there, they were confident in their ability to fortify it. However, the surviving units were terribly disorganized, with companies separated from regiments, regiments separated from brigades, and brigades separated from divisions. For more than an hour, the Army of the Potomac resembled little more than a disorganized mob. So recalled a Wisconsin colonel, "If fresh troops had attacked us then, we unquestionably would have fared badly. The troops were scattered over the hill in much disorder, while a stream of stragglers and wounded men pushed along the Baltimore Turnpike toward the rear." Many regiments were mere skeletons. The chaplain of the 94th New York explained, "On average, less than ¼ of those who went into action three hours before, made their appearance now! How sad we felt when we saw who and how many were not present you can better imagine than I describe! Our Colonel, 5 Captains, 4 Lieutenants and 275 of our brave boys were among the missing."

But order soon emerged. Although several officers helped to organize the routed men, Maj. Gen. Winfield S. Hancock received the most credit. Hancock had no affiliation with either the 1st or 11th Corps. At 1 p.m., when word of Reynolds's death reached the Army of the Potomac's headquarters at Taneytown, Meade instructed Hancock, who commanded the 2nd Corps, to leave his unit, head to Gettysburg, and "assume command of the corps there assembled." Around 4.30 p.m., Hancock arrived at Cemetery Hill, and after a brief consultation with Howard, he took charge. By most accounts, the meeting was prickly. Howard was senior to Hancock and probably considered it an affront to have another officer relieve him of command in the midst of a battle. As Howard later told it, he and Hancock agreed to share authority, with Howard directing the right of the line and Hancock the left. Whatever Howard believed, most accounts confirm that Hancock took charge *in effect*. A sergeant in the 147th New York later clarified the importance of Hancock's leadership: "Hancock sat his horse, superb and calm as on review; imperturbable, self-reliant, as if the fate of the battle and of the nation were not his to decide. It almost led us to doubt whether there had been cause for retreat at all. His dispositions were prompt … No excitement in voice or manner, only cool, concise, and positive directions, given in a steady voice and a conversational tone."

Hancock exuded steadiness largely because reinforcements conveniently arrived when he did. An Indiana regiment that had been guarding the 1st Corps wagon trains showed up, adding 434 fresh troops to the mix. By 5

Major General Winfield Scott Hancock commanded the Army of the Potomac's 2nd Corps. At 1 p.m., Meade gave him orders to head to Gettysburg and assume command of all troops on the field and direct the defense until Meade arrived. Hancock reached the field at 4:30 p.m. and began rallying the routed troops atop Cemetery Hill. According to several witnesses, Hancock's determined demeanor restored a fighting spirit to several broken regiments. (NARA)

This photograph taken by Timothy O'Sullivan on July 7, depicts the Evergreen Cemetery Gatehouse along the Baltimore Pike. At 4:45 p.m., this was the location where Hancock, Howard, and Doubleday gathered to rally the shattered remains of 1st Corps and 11th Corps. By 6 p.m., the Union generals had patched together a strong defensive line. (NARA)

p.m., Hancock learned that the 12th Corps was on hand, another 9,780 aggregate. That corps had started the day at Littlestown, eleven miles to the southeast. At noon, while the 12th Corps was paused at Two Taverns, the corps commander, Maj. Gen. Henry W. Slocum, had received news of the battle. He ordered his men to traverse the remaining five miles. The 12th Corps' advance was unusually slow on July 1—about one mile per hour—and consequently, the corps had no influence on the outcome of the first day's fight. But it arrived in time to shore up defenses. Hancock also had the assistance of Col. Orland Smith's brigade, the only 11th Corps brigade not committed to the action north of town. Altogether, Hancock probably had 17,000 officers and men available.

Like Howard, Hancock appreciated the importance of Cemetery Hill and he chose to reinforce it. Once they rallied, the 11th Corps troops held positions along the north side of the Evergreen Cemetery, facing Gettysburg. Hancock ordered Wadsworth's decimated 1st Division, 1st Corps, to extend that line to the east, taking possession of another suitable peak, this one called Culp's Hill. Doubleday's other divisions, the 2nd and 3rd, formed on the left flank of the 11th Corps, extending its line south along Cemetery Ridge, the southern spur of Cemetery Hill. Once the 12th Corps arrived, Hancock sent one of its divisions—Brig. Gen. John Geary's 2nd Division—to the left of Doubleday's men. Geary's men anchored the Union flank at two rocky hills known as Little Round Top and Big Round Top. The other division of the 12th Corps—Brig. Gen. Alpheus Williams's 1st Division—moved to the opposite flank. It crossed Rock Creek and held a lofty hill that overlooked the town from its east side. This was called Benner's Hill, astride the Hanover Road.

In an hour's time, the Army of the Potomac cobbled together another impressive defense. The new line extended about two miles, covered two important avenues of advance—the Baltimore Pike and the Taneytown Road—and it had the advantage of sloping ground with a clear field of fire. Everywhere, exhausted Union soldiers continued to pitch in. Lieut. Col. Rufus Dawes noticed how, without prompting, his soldiers grabbed shovels from the nearby regimental wagons and diligently entrenched the slopes of Culp's Hill. "The men worked with great energy," Dawes later wrote. "A man would dig with all his strength until out of breath, when another would seize the spade and push on the work. There were no orders to construct these breastworks, but the situation plainly dictated their necessity."

Not far away, the Army of Northern Virginia contemplated its next move. Worn out by the costly attacks or broken by the chaotic progress through the town, the four Confederate divisions involved in the pursuit halted and formed defensive lines. Rodes's division took position on the south side of Gettysburg. They grabbed furniture from houses and barricaded the streets. Having fought since 7 a.m., Pettigrew's division pulled back to Herr's Ridge for a much-needed rest and resupply. Meanwhile, Pender's division, still licking its wounds, halted atop Seminary Ridge, taking care to watch for the approach of Federal troops along the Fairfield Road. Early's division reformed on the fields east of Gettysburg, guarding the approaches along the York and Hanover roads. Finally, a fifth division began arriving on the field: Maj. Gen. Edward Johnson's division of Ewell's corps, 6,430 fresh troops. These men arrived via the Mummasburg Road. They cut across the north end of town and moved toward the Confederate left flank. Ewell expected to have these troops at the front by 8 p.m.

As the sun began to set, Robert E. Lee took stock of the situation. He had seen very little of the combat on July 1, arriving in time only to witness Pender's attack. During the Union retreat, Lee rode along the Chambersburg Pike and ordered his staff to pitch tents near the Mary Thompson house. After that, he rode south to the Theological Seminary. At this point, perhaps 5.30 p.m., Lieut. Gen. Longstreet rode up. His troops, who had been marching all day, were then reaching Marsh Creek, back where the battle began, four miles away. As Longstreet told it, after observing the Union position with Lee, he suggested repositioning the army on better ground—which meant abandoning Gettysburg altogether. Attempting to cajole his commander, Longstreet said, "All we have to do is file around his left and secure good ground between him and his capital." Not responding to Longstreet's advice directly, Lee replied, "If the enemy is there tomorrow, we must attack him." To convey the importance of continuing the attack, Lee thrust his fist in the direction of Cemetery Hill. Longstreet rejoined, "If he is there tomorrow it will be because he wants you to attack."

Trying to calm Lee, Longstreet suggested that if the heights south of town were so important, the army should attack them at once. Heeding this guidance, Lee sent one of his staff officers to carry verbal instructions to Ewell, encouraging him to attack the heights south of town "if practicable," but also, at the same time and quite contradictorily, not to bring on a general engagement. Not knowing the names of the hills, Lee simply called them the "heights," hoping Ewell would get the gist. The messenger, Walter Taylor, dashed through town and encountered Ewell near the "Diamond," Gettysburg's version of a town square. The dialogue passed quickly and Taylor reported that he left with "the impression upon my mind" that Ewell would execute the attack.

Undoubtedly, Ewell understood the target of Lee's request. Lee wanted him to attack Cemetery Hill, the center of the Union army's new line. Accordingly, Ewell accompanied his divisional commanders to the skirmish line in front of Rodes's division. They were not there long when a few stray

Lieut. Gen. James Longstreet arrived on the field at 5 p.m., ahead of his troops. He witnessed the final moments of Pender's assault and conferred with Lee. When Lee insisted that the army continue the battle the next day, Longstreet advised making a night assault to secure either Cemetery Hill or Culp's Hill. Although Lee agreed with him, no night assault ever emerged. (Library of Congress)

This photograph depicts the Mary Thompson house on July 15, 1863. This building served as Lee's headquarters on July 2 and 3. Although Lee likely slept inside the dwelling, he conducted official business from a tent erected outside the house. On July 1, Union infantry and artillery had made a desperate stand in the fields on both sides of the house. When Lee arrived on the scene an hour later, he conferred with Longstreet and emphatically stated his intent to continue battle on the fields south of town. "If the enemy is there tomorrow," Lee declared, "we must attack him." (Library of Congress)

shots from the Union position convinced them to return to the safety of the Diamond. Next, a confusing report reached Ewell. One of his brigade commanders, Brig. Gen. William Smith, reported the presence of Union troops along the York Road. Some of Smith's scouts had seen Williams's 12th Corps division along the Hanover Road. Then, someone had confused the road names, so when the report reached Ewell, he had no idea from which direction he should be concerned. Ewell paused combat operations until this intelligence got sorted out. However, by that point, Ewell became convinced he could not assail Cemetery Hill without a dramatic loss of life. He sent two staff officers on a reconnaissance mission, telling them to scout nearby Culp's Hill, to see if that peak could be taken instead. The staff officers did not get far but they reported—quite incorrectly—that Culp's Hill was unoccupied.

According to several witnesses, Ewell's divisional commanders encouraged him to advance as soon as Johnson's division reached the east side of town. Jubal Early warned, "If you do not go up there tonight, it will cost you ten thousand men to get up there tomorrow." This advice had little effect. At some point during the evening, Ewell elected to do nothing, a decision that earned him censure from many postwar historians. Ewell's caution may have been warranted. The presence of Wadsworth's division along the northern slope of Culp's Hill and the location of Williams's division to the east of the hill rendered a night assault doubtful. Ewell did not know the exact dispositions of the enemy, but he had enough acumen to assume that an attack against Culp's Hill, launched at whatever hour, would be more difficult than the assaults against Oak Ridge and Blocher's Knoll. Further, despite what others have contended, Lee's directives to Ewell were discretionary, not absolute. At no point did Lee exhibit displeasure with Ewell's caution. Neither of them, it seems, understood the new Union position, nor how many men they ought to commit to a possible attack.

After dark, Lee rode to Ewell's headquarters, probably the John S. Crawford house, to ponder the next day's action. Rodes and Early were also present, and the four generals conversed for over an hour. Initially, Lee exhibited an eagerness to continue the fight. But after hearing Ewell's stated objections to the proposed night assault, Lee asked if Ewell's corps could attack the next day, "as early as possible," in the same area. Neither Ewell, nor Rodes, nor Early endorsed this. They all suggested that an attack against the other flank—the Union left—would be more suitable. Grumbling, Lee pointed out that this required him to wait for Longstreet's corps. He could not expect an assault against the Union left until well after daybreak. It frustrated Lee to give the Army of the Potomac another lull—precious time to improve its position—but Lee followed the advice of his generals. Accordingly, he called off any further attacks until Longstreet was ready. With that, the battle of July 1 came to a close.

NIGHTFALL

As night fell, the two armies took stock of their situation. For both sides, casualty figures were just short of apocalyptic. Confederate losses stood at 5,634, a mix of killed, wounded, and missing. Complicating the Army of Northern Virginia's logistical nightmare, all the wounded were scattered. Via ambulance or ambulation, Confederate medical personnel had collected or directed wounded men to dozens of nearby structures. By day's end, some thirty farms or public buildings were occupied by Confederate patients, and these were scattered across an arc six miles wide.

Hastily, Confederate soldiers buried their dead on the fields where they had fallen. Soldiers had no time for reflection or prayer, nor could they ensure that families could recover the remains. In the fields near the Forney farm, Lieut. Henry Macon led a squad to bury Capt. William C. Ousby of the 43rd North Carolina. Ousby's comrades placed a wooden headboard at his grave, with his name, rank, and regiment scratched into it. Macon wrote,

At the corner of York and Stratton Streets, 33-year-old Sgt. Amos Humiston of Company C, 154th New York, died clutching an ambrotype of his three children: Franklin, Alice, and Frederick. When a Philadelphia physician learned of the story, he publicized the image of "Gettysburg's unknown soldier" to determine his identity. Eventually, Humiston's widow, Philinda, came forward identifying herself as the mother of the three children in the photograph. In the autumn, Humiston's body was laid to rest inside the Soldier's National Cemetery. This illustration incorrectly places Humiston's body in an open field (and not inside the town) but it correctly shows the position he was in when he was found, with ambrotype clutched to his chest. (Library of Congress)

AN INCIDENT OF GETTYSBURG—THE LAST THOUGHT OF A DYING FATHER.

The positions of the armies at nightfall on the first day

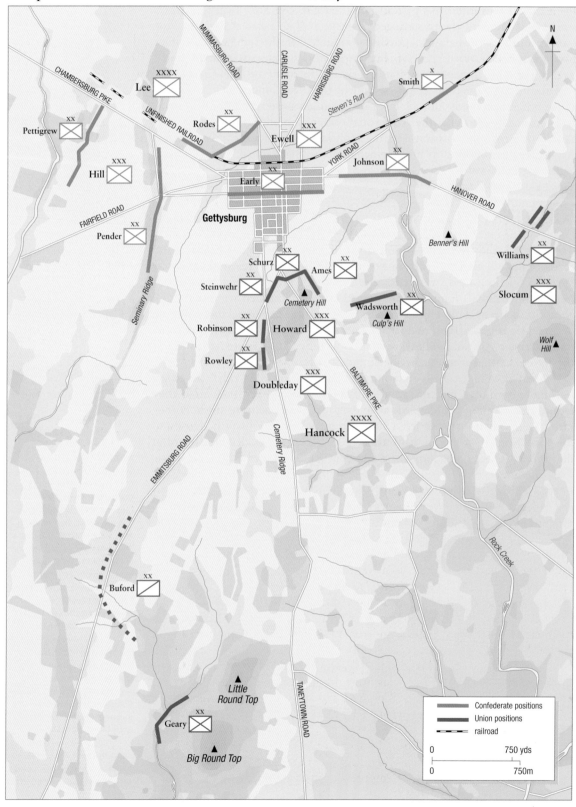

"[T]his was the best that could be done for him." Sometime after the battle, the gravesite was lost. Ousby's body was never recovered.

Also, Confederate forces bagged about 2,500 prisoners. Woefully unprepared to feed them, the provost battalions hastily marched the prisoners out of harm's way. Initially, the guards held them at Marsh Creek. For many of them, this was the beginning of a long, hellish experience that ended in misery, suffering, and death. Pvt. James Bailey, an 11th Corps soldier who had been captured in town, wrote that, as he settled down in the grass to get some sleep, there was "a strange stillness pervading the air." Bailey could not shake a dark feeling churning in his stomach. He continued: "But there was something quite oppressive in the unnatural quiet that reigned. I felt that many forms were moving about at no great distance—that heavy columns were forming for a terrible struggle, and that Death was making his grim preparations for a horrible feast. Alas! that human passions should so triumph over human pity. It could hardly seem possible that those bright stars were shining down on men plotting and thirsting for fellow blood. Yet I knew it to be so, and bemoaning the cause that should beget such a necessity, I muttered a prayer for mercy, and fell asleep."

Shortly before midnight, Lee returned to the Thompson house. His conference with Ewell, Rodes, and Early had given him much to consider. *Where should he attack tomorrow? Should he even attack at all?* Of the former question, Lee had several hours to consider his options. Of the latter, Lee did not deliberate for long. In his post-battle report, Lee explained that he had little choice but to continue the fight, as it had become "in a measure, unavoidable." Lee fretted he could not withdraw west to the mountains, not with all his supply trains choking up the roads. Nor could he expect to forage in the presence of the enemy. Whether these excuses came from an honest mind or not, Lee convinced himself that he needed to continue the battle. Writing clumsily in the passive voice, Lee concluded, "Encouraged by the successful issue of the engagement of the first day, and in view of the valuable results that would ensue from the defeat of the army of General Meade, it was thought advisable to renew the attack." In a postwar account, Lee's staff officer, Taylor, summed up the situation crisply: "Having failed to reap the full fruit of the victory before night, his mind was occupied with the idea of renewing the assault upon the enemy with the dawn of the day on the 2d." However Lee rendered it, he made an important decision at that moment. The Battle of Gettysburg would last *at least* one more day.

Union losses on the first day amounted to 8,955 killed, wounded, and missing. Most of the wounded and nearly all of the dead had been left in enemy hands. Behind Union lines, the Army of the Potomac established new field hospitals to accommodate those who had been evacuated. The 1st Corps operated at the Nicholas Mark "White Church" and at the farms owned by Isaac Lightner, Peter Conover, and Jesse Young. Meanwhile, the 11th Corps occupied the George Spangler farm. Also, Union forces captured about 1,000 Confederates. These prisoners were marched out of the area, taken to Westminster and eventually sent on a path that took them to Point Lookout, Maryland. Like their Union counterparts, they began a laborious journey of misery that did not end until the war's conclusion in 1865, or earlier if they died in captivity.

Lieutenant Colonel Henry Shippen Huidekoper of the 150th Pennsylvania received two gunshot wounds during the fighting at the Edward McPherson barn, one of which shattered his right elbow. He made his way into town and at the St. Francis Xavier Church on High Street, a surgeon amputated his right arm. "The night was a horrible one," Huidekoper remembered. "All night long I heard from downstairs moans, groans, and shrieks, and yells from the wounded and suffering soldiers." In 1905, he received the Medal of Honor for his performance at Gettysburg. For the remainder of his life, he dreamed of his missing arm, and even at age 67, he admitted that, in his dreams, "I remain a man with a perfect frame." (*History of the One Hundred and Fiftieth Regiment, Pennsylvania Volunteers. Second Regiment, Bucktail Brigade*, 1895)

During the first day of the battle, Maj. Alexander W. Biddle's horse, Transportation, was struck by three rifle balls, which caused him to gallop off the field, leaving Biddle stranded near the Seminary. At sunset, Biddle and Transportation were reunited when the horse appeared atop the crest of Cemetery Hill, carrying one of Brig. Gen. Buford's orderlies. The reunion of horse and rider reinvigorated Biddle, who felt certain that the Army of the Potomac would win the battle. "There is no doubt of success," Biddle wrote that evening. "May God guide us and be merciful to us." (*History of the 121st Regiment Pennsylvania Volunteers*, 1905)

At Taneytown, the new army commander, George Meade, made an important decision. He elected to defend Gettysburg. Although several subordinate commanders—Buford, Reynolds, Doubleday, Howard, and Hancock—had played a role in bringing the battle to Gettysburg, Meade still held the option of pulling his embattled troops back to Pipe Creek. At some point during the day, he discarded that option. In the late afternoon, Hancock sent a message, informing Meade that the terrain south of Gettysburg could be defended. If Meade wished to hold it, Hancock said, he should hurry to Gettysburg with the rest of the army. Meade had already made the decision to concentrate at Gettysburg before Hancock's message arrived, but this assurance gave him confidence. At 10 p.m., he ordered his staff to mount up and head for Cemetery Hill, where he intended to meet Hancock and the other corps commanders. They had fourteen miles to go.

As daylight faded on July 1, another Union officer trudged his way onto Cemetery Hill. Maj. Alexander W. Biddle had been abruptly dismounted atop McPherson's Ridge when his beloved horse, Transportation, was wounded in the neck. Although Biddle's regiment had been all but annihilated by its "last stand" at the Seminary, Biddle survived unhurt. Separated from his brigade during the retreat, he followed the throng of exhausted infantry through the streets of Gettysburg and somehow avoided capture. Parched and weary, he reached the Evergreen Cemetery gatehouse. There, he heard a familiar whinny. Turning around, Biddle saw his cherished horse, Transportation, standing there to greet him. After fleeing the field, Transportation had presented himself to a friendly Union cavalryman, who, in turn, handed him over to a dismounted orderly. Now, in the darkening gloom, Transportation let out an enthusiastic neigh. Horse and rider were reunited!

Happily, Maj. Biddle remounted. Through the smoke, he and Transportation found their regiment, or what was left of it. Sixty-six survivors from the 121st Pennsylvania were huddled underneath a tattered banner. When Biddle saw them, a strange indefinable emotion welled up inside of him. It was not despair, as he initially supposed, but *hope*. The scene was etched into Biddle's memory. Transportation was still bleeding, but having shaken off the shock of his wound, he was ready for a second round. All around them, the 1st Corps soldiers busily prepared their defenses. The soldiers of Biddle's regiment—the two-legged and the four-legged—were ready for more. Minutes later, Biddle wrote this: "I have reason to thank God for my merciful preservation and I trust the obstinacy of the fight will be emulated by the other Corps … [T]here is no doubt of success. As we marched up the hill in the Evening a beautiful rainbow spanned the Eastern sky. I hailed it as a sign of promise for I believe if ever men fought under a sense of duty, all do so now. May God guide us and be merciful to us."

Biddle's sobering confidence was not misplaced. As the next two days demonstrated, the Army of the Potomac was, indeed, ready to fight.

THE BATTLEFIELD TODAY

The majority of the land upon which the first day's engagement took place is protected by Gettysburg National Military Park (GNMP). GNMP grounds are accessible to the public free of charge. From April to October, the battlefield is open from 6 a.m. to 10 p.m. During the remaining months, the park closes at 7 p.m. Nearly all areas where heavy fighting occurred are accessible on foot; however, the battlefield is vast and separated by rough terrain. Visitors should expect to travel from place to place along the National Park Service's paved roads, most of which are one way. Four prescribed auto-tour "stops" (described in GNMP's official brochure) encompass the first day's field: McPherson's Ridge, the Eternal Peace Light Memorial, Oak Ridge, and Barlow (Blocher's) Knoll.

Meanwhile, the road network of the historic borough—which is independent of the park—is largely unchanged. Currently, Gettysburg and the surrounding countryside contain more than 300 1863-era dwellings, some of which still bear the scars of battle.

Some important sites are located on private property. For instance, the "First Shot Marker" is on an isolated sliver of NPS property adjacent to a private residence. Coster Avenue—the current name for where Charles Coster's brigade made its forlorn stand on the afternoon of July 1—consists of a grassy walkway owned by the NPS which directly abuts the backyards of several private dwellings. The Herr Tavern—the site where Lee paused to deliberate Hill's advance—is now a dining establishment. Certain historic farm houses also function as park service administration buildings or are cared for by NPS staff. A private museum—the Seminary Ridge Museum—occupies the ground of the Lutheran Theological Seminary. Visitors should be respectful of private property and mindful of the operating hours of private businesses.

In addition to Gettysburg, other battlefields from the campaign are also preserved. The battlefield of Brandy Station contains 1,800 acres of land maintained by the American Battlefield Trust and its partner, the Brandy Station Foundation. The bulk of the battlefield is accessible via walking trails.

The battlefield of Hanover is virtually vanished, although several monuments, historic markers, and waysides interpret the battle. Finally, there are more than forty waysides spread across Virginia, Maryland, and Pennsylvania maintained by the Civil War Trails organization. These markers follow and interpret the Confederate invasion and the Union pursuit.

BIBLIOGRAPHY

Beck, Brandon H. and Charles S. Grunder. *The Second Battle of Winchester, June 12–15, 1863.* Lynchburg, Virginia: H. E. Howard, Inc., 1989.

Biddle, Chapman. *The First Day of the Battle of Gettysburg.* Philadelphia, Pennsylvania: J. B. Lippencott, 1880.

Brown, Kent Masterson. *Meade at Gettysburg: A Study in Command.* Chapel Hill, North Carolina: University Press of North Carolina, 2021.

Coco, Gregory A. *A Strange and Blighted Land, Gettysburg: The Aftermath of Battle.* Gettysburg, Pennsylvania: Thomas Publications, 1995.

Coddington, Edwin B. *The Gettysburg Campaign: A Study in Command.* New York: Charles Scribner's Sons, 1968.

Frassanito, William A. *Gettysburg: A Journey in Time.* Gettysburg, Pennsylvania: Thomas Publications, 1975.

Gallagher, Gary W. (ed.). *The First Day at Gettysburg: Essays on Confederate and Union Leadership.* Kent, Ohio: Kent State University Press, 1992.

Gottfried, Bradley M. *The Maps of the Cavalry in the Gettysburg Campaign: An Atlas of Mounted Operations from Brandy Station through Falling Waters, June 9–July 14, 1863.* El Dorado Hills, California: Savas Beatie, 2020.

Guelzo, Allen C. *Gettysburg: The Last Invasion.* New York: Vintage Books, 2013.

Harman, Troy D. "In Defense of Henry Slocum on July 1," in D. Scott Hartwig (ed.), *I Ordered No Man to Go Where I Would Not Go Myself: Leadership in the Campaign and Battle of Gettysburg, Papers of the Ninth Gettysburg National Military Park Seminar.* Gettysburg, Pennsylvania: National Park Service, 2002.

Hartwig, D. Scott. "'Never Have I Seen Such a Charge': Pender's Light Division at Gettysburg, July 1," in Hartwig (ed.), *The High Water Mark: The Army of Northern Virginia in the Gettysburg Campaign, Programs of the Seventh Annual Gettysburg Seminar.* Gettysburg, Pennsylvania: National Park Service, 1999.

Hartwig, D. Scott (ed.). *This Has Been A Terrible Ordeal: The Gettysburg Campaign and First Day of Battle, Papers of the Ninth Gettysburg National Military Park Seminar.* Gettysburg, Pennsylvania: National Park Service, 2005.

Hassler, Jr., Warren W. *Crisis at the Crosswords: The First Day at Gettysburg.* Tuscaloosa, Alabama: University of Alabama Press, 1970.

Herdegen, Lance J., and William J. K. Beaudot. *In the Bloody Railroad Cut at Gettysburg.* Dayton, Ohio: Morningside Press, 1990.

Ladd, David L. and Audrey J. Ladd. *The Bachelder Papers: Gettysburg in Their Own Words, Volumes 1–3.* Dayton, Ohio: Morningside House, Inc., 1995.

Mackowski, Chris, Kristopher D. White, and Daniel T. Davis. *Fight Like the Devil: The First Day at Gettysburg, July 1, 1863.* El Dorado Hills, California: Savas Beatie, 2015.

Martin, David G. *Gettysburg July 1* (revised edition). Conshohocken, Pennsylvania: Combined Books, 1996.

Newton, Steven H. *McPherson's Ridge: The First Battle for the High Ground, July 1, 1863.* Cambridge, Massachusetts: DaCapo Press, 2002.

Pfanz, Harry W. *Gettysburg—Culp's Hill and Cemetery Hill.* Chapel Hill, North Carolina: University Press of North Carolina, 1993.

Pfanz, Harry W. *Gettysburg—The First Day.* Chapel Hill, North Carolina: University Press of North Carolina, 2001.

Pryor, Elizabeth Brown. *Reading the Man: A Portrait of Robert E. Lee through his Private Letters.* New York: Penguin Books, 2007.

Reardon, Carol and Tom Vossler. *A Field Guide to Gettysburg: Experiencing the Battlefield through its History, Places, and People.* Chapel Hill, North Carolina: University of North Carolina Press, 2013.

Sears, Stephen. *Gettysburg.* New York: Houghton Mifflin Company, 2003.

Shue, Richard S. *Morning at Willoughby Run: The Opening Battle at Gettysburg July 1, 1863.* Gettysburg, Pennsylvania: Thomas Publications, 1998.

Trudeau, Noah Andre. *Gettysburg: A Testing of Courage.* New York: Harper-Collins, 2002.

U.S. War Department, *The War of the Rebellion: A Compilation of the Official Records of the Union and Confederate Armies, Series 1, Volume 27, Parts 1–3.* Washington, D.C.: Government Printing Office, 1889.

Wittenberg, Eric J. *The Battle of Brandy Station: North America's Largest Cavalry Battle.* Charleston, South Carolina: The History Press, 2010.

Wittenberg, Eric J. *"The Devil's to Pay": John Buford at Gettysburg, a History and Walking Tour.* El Dorado Hills, California: Savas Beatie, 2014.

Woodworth, Steven E. *Beneath a Northern Sky: A Short History of the Gettysburg Campaign.* Wilmington, Delaware: Scholarly Resources, Inc., 2003.

INDEX

Figures in **bold** refer to illustrations.